BRIAN
THE FANS BEH

G000068227

BY STEVE BROOKES

EMPIRE
PUBLICATIONS

First published in 2015

EMPIRE PUBLICATIONS

1 Newton Street, Manchester M1 1HW

Printed in Great Britain.

CONTENTS

FOREWORD
BY JOHN McGOVERN

HAVING WORKED FOR BRIAN CLOUGH for approximately fifteen years I can honestly say he was the easiest person to work for in football, providing you were prepared to give 100% towards getting a result for the ninety minutes of a game.

Throughout my career I was often criticised with possessing no pace – true. Not being a good header of the ball – true. Not being a good tackler – true. Not scoring many goals - also true. Why then did Brian Clough put such trust in me, making me captain of Nottingham Forest as we won the Football League Championship, two Football League Cups and two European Cups?

Primarily because he was a genius in recognising the important skills required to win football matches and the importance of intelligent players who understood the game. The ability of being able to control and pass the ball consistently and accurately far outweigh the pace, strength, and aggression at the forefront in many modern coaches' minds.

Knowing where the ball is going before it comes to you

is a gift I was fortunate to possess. Brian Clough alongside Peter Taylor brought success to football clubs quicker than any other management team in the history of football and it was a privilege to have been appreciated by them.

INTRODUCTION

WHEN A NOTTINGHAM FOREST fan uses the phrase 'met God', you would normally think that they were talking about the creative and combative midfielder who graced the City Ground in the 1980s. Dutchman Johnny Metgod has his own place in Forest folklore thanks to a free-kick he scored from long range against West Ham in 1985. The ball flew unstoppably past Phil Parkes into the roof of the net and Metgod celebrated by waggling his finger in the air, a gesture reminiscent of Dennis Taylor's famous celebration in the World Snooker Championships final of the same year. It still occasionally features in compilations of great goals, and is talked about by supporters of a certain age who remember those special days in Nottingham.

However, when I use the words 'met God', the God to whom I refer is that most revered and special of football managers, Brian Clough.

It is impossible to write too much about Nottingham Forest, or, indeed, their mortal enemies, Derby County, without the subject turning to the great man. His aura is always felt at both football clubs, and forever will be. Before him, both teams had struggled for years, and were regarded as also-rans who would never threaten the dominance of the more fashionable sides. After him, both clubs have enjoyed only brief highlights among difficult seasons of underachievement. But during his time in charge, he won very nearly everything there was to win, and reached heights it would have been impossible to imagine either club attaining under any other manager. Indeed, if Nottingham Forest had won the FA Cup when they reached the final in 1991, he would pretty much have swept the board (as opposed to taking much pleasure in alienating them, as he did for most of his career).

Brian Clough is a hero to many people throughout the East Midlands and the wider footballing world. He has been a personal idol ever since I first began to enjoy, and endure, the highs and lows of supporting a football team as a young boy. So when I learned that he was signing copies of his autobiography, Cloughie: Walking on Water, at ASDA in Spondon, Derbyshire, I just knew that I had to go.

My brother and I arrived shortly before the advertised time, knowing that it would be busy. We were more than happy to queue patiently for the chance of meeting him, but we hadn't reckoned on just how popular the event would be. By the time we arrived, the queue was already stretching from the table where Brian was sitting, up and down the aisle back to the entrance, and spilling out into the car-park. Nonetheless, we took our place behind all the other hopeful fans and kept our fingers crossed that the queue would move with sufficient speed that we might reach the front before the time came for him to leave.

Unfortunately, news came that he was on a tight schedule, and we were still a long way from the point where the queue had been asked to disband by one of the store-workers who was acting as a steward for the event. She politely told us that there was no point waiting any longer and we were devastated. The dream was over. We'd been in the same room as our idol, we'd seen him from a short distance, but we were to be denied the chance to get any closer, to exchange words with him, and to obtain an autograph that we could cherish forever. We were gutted.

That's when fate, or maybe even that other God, smiled down on us. A little earlier in the day, we had noticed that among the group standing near to Brian was his long time assistant, Ronnie Fenton. There are two things with which my brother and I associated Ronnie. Firstly, he used to be quoted on the local sports news at least two or three times a season declaring that a story that Forest had been linked with possibly buying a new player was 'absolute rubbish' or that there was 'no truth in it at all.' Invariably, we would then sign the player a week or two later. It was designed to throw people off the scent, or to make sure we didn't have to pay over the odds but for experienced Fenton observers it was an amusing game to read between the lines. And the second thing we associated him with was his daughter. In my brother's first week at university, he had mentioned to one of his lecturers that he was a Forest fan, and his lecturer informed him that another tutor on the same course was Ron Fenton's daughter. This news, naturally, delighted him, but he had never envisaged that it would eventually pay such a dividend.

My brother, encouraged by me, walked shyly over to where Fenton was standing and introduced himself. They chatted for a few minutes and my brother's abiding memory is of what a lovely, welcoming and friendly man he was. He took his leave and returned to join the queue, the queue which we were to learn about twenty minutes or so later that we would never reach the front of.

We were about to trudge disappointedly back to the car when I suggested that we hang around for a while. As the massed ranks headed for the exits, we idly browsed the magazines and CDs in the racks near the cigarette counter. As the crowd thinned out, Brian and his cortege started to walk to the exit. I suggested to my brother that he should utilise his newly formed friendship with his lecturer's father to try and sneak us a quick word with Brian. He was slightly reluctant but headed over and asked whether there was any chance of perhaps saying a quick hello to Brian. Perhaps it is my memory playing tricks but I could swear that the terrible supermarket music was interrupted briefly by the Hallelujah Chorus, as he said 'yes, no problem', and ushered us past the last of the stragglers and into the orbit of our Messiah.

Brian was being led towards the exit but Ron stopped him for a moment and introduced us as 'two of my daughter's pupils'. A slight inaccuracy but we weren't about to correct him. My brother was the first to walk towards Brian, his legs trembling and said: 'It's a great pleasure to meet you.' They then shook hands as Brian said it was nice to meet him too. I decided to chance my arm and say a bit more, a decision which almost led to disaster.

For years, I had been sending Brian a Christmas card and Brian and his wife Barbara had always sent me one in return. In fact, some years the Cloughs sent their cards before I'd even had the chance to send mine. So I introduced myself by saying: 'Hello, Brian. I'm Jamie, I send you a Christmas card every year.' Brian wasn't in the best of health at this time. It was a few months before his liver operation, the operation which made him look and sound so much healthier and more vibrant in his last couple of years. Before the operation, though, he was quite shaky, and I think his hearing must have been suffering a bit too, as he replied: 'You want me to send you a Christmas card?' I instantly broke out in a cold sweat.

The greatest moment in my life to date, the meeting I'd always dreamed of and it was about to become one of those horrible moments that must never be spoken of. The dream had become a nightmare.

We should have had no such worries. The Hallelujah

Chorus rang out once more, as I said: 'No, you already do send me one, I send you one too,' to which Brian replied: 'Oh, you're that Jamie,' and prodded me lightly just above the stomach as a gesture of recognition. Whether he did really know me by name or not we'll never actually know for sure, of course but just by doing that, by making that little gesture, he made me feel about 10 feet tall. It was a perfect moment, just as we'd hoped it would be. A few words, a couple of handshakes, a friendly punch in the stomach, and we were the two happiest men in the world for the rest of that day, week and month.

On my way home, I sent a text to a friend to tell him that I'd just met God. He read my message and thought I'd been involved in a car-crash and had some sort of near-death experience. I might have hoped that, rather than thinking I'd just wrapped a car round a lamp-post, he'd have read 'met God' and thought I'd just crashed in a 35 yard free-kick before celebrating like a joyous Northern Irish master of the baize. Alas, he knows my meagre footballing skills too well to have made that mistake. I told him the story of our meeting with the great man, and, as a lifelong Forest fan himself, he was suitably impressed. And it made me think.

We've heard so many stories about Cloughie. Hilarious stories, stories of achievement and hubris and unorthodox methods, of extraordinary generosity and terrifying unpredictability. We've read his own words in his autobiography, and watched his interviews, which were always entertaining, forthright and never towed any party lines. We've heard from journalists whose job it was to coax these interviews from him; sometimes a very easy task, sometimes nigh on impossible. We've heard much from the people who played for him, who are always happy to share tales of his often bizarre approach to management, and his ability to get the very best out of those who might otherwise not have fulfilled their potential. But we've never really heard from the fans. The ordinary people like my brother and I, who happened across him in everyday life and went away with a story that we will tell forever.

In the following pages, we hear from people who were lucky enough to meet him throughout the years. Even the briefest moments spent in his company were enough to create stories that will be passed on through generations. These are stories from people who witnessed, firsthand, this unique man in action.

People who are fortunate enough to be able to say: 'This is the story of the day I met Brian Clough.'

Jamie Hastie

THE FANS BEHIND THE LEGEND

A DECENT PROPOSAL

I WROTE TO FOREST and asked if I could propose over the electriconic scoreboards during one of their stadium tours. The lady was very helpful and helped me sort everything out. We would arrive at the ground early and she would then take us through to the seats in the main stand. The man who works the electric scoreboard would wait for me to scratch my head, he would then set the score boards off showing my proposal. Everything would work like clockwork she assured me.

Everything would have as well if it hadn't have been for a certain twist of fate. Just as we pulled into the City Ground car park we saw a Mercedes car just outside the reception, as we got out of our car and walked over to the reception, I froze as I saw Cloughie stood in the doorway with a cameraman. To say I was star struck was a complete understatement. I couldn't believe it. We looked through the door where we could see Brian stood with our then manager David Platt having their photo taken with the new statue of Brian that had just been unveiled. I got my camera out and told my intended, Samantha, I was going to ask if I could have my photo taken with them both. I waited while the film crew had finished then I cheekily asked if I could have my picture taken with them.

'Is this lovely lady taking the photo your wife' said Cloughie.

'Not yet' I replied.

'Well I'm not having my picture taken with you unless I can have it with both of you' he said smiling.

The TV cameraman then took the camera from Sam and we both stood with Brian while the cameraman snapped away. I was totally awestruck, I couldn't believe it. I then got a photo with just Brian, David Platt and myself. (Me with the best ever and the worst ever Forest managers in history, sorry Platty) it was turning out to be an unbelievable day and I hadn't even done what we came here for yet.

After about ten minutes of talking to us Cloughie went off to do a TV interview. We then went over to the lady on reception and I gave her my name. 'Oh you are a little early' she said. 'Would you like to go and wait in the director's box and I will come and get you when everybody else arrives,' she said.

We walked up the stairs and sat in the seats in the director's box.

'What's up with you, you silly bugger,' said Sam, 'you're smiling like a lunatic, It's only Cloughie.'

'Nothing' I said as I scratched my head. The scoreboard lit up immediately!

'I've something to ask you' I said pointing to the scoreboard. Now it was Sam's turn to be gobsmacked.

'*SAM I LOVE YOU WILL YOU MARRY ME?*' Flashed up on the scoreboard.

I think it was the last thing on earth she expected and I wasn't quite sure what she was going to say. Luckily for me, she didn't leave me feeling like a total loser and she said yes. We sat in the stands for a while staring at the pitch, me chuffed to bits and Sam confused at what had just happened to her. The lady from reception then came up to us and led us inside. We were taken into the manager's office where a bottle of champagne was waiting for us with a good luck message from Brian. We were treated like royalty for the next half an hour. It was an absolutely amazing day that we will both never forget. What a day! Just don't ask me which I was more excited about!!

A week later I sent my photographs to Brian's house in Quarndon asking him if he would be so kind as to sign them for us, and within a week he had sent them back beautifully signed personally to the both of us.

They are very precious to us and are a lasting reminder of our very special day.

Johnny Royle

I WAS ABOUT 7 OR 8, which would've made it about 1987/88. Myself, my father and my friend Darren were at a Forest reserve game when just after half time a gentleman with a Labrador dog sat in front of us. The game wasn't exactly thrilling and with my friend Darren not being a football fan (come to think of it I'm not too sure why he came!) he started to play eye spy (or is it I-spy) with the advertising hoardings. After about 10 minutes of trying to guess his "L" I turned to him and said, "You making this up? There isn't one with an L".

A second gentleman, who we hadn't noticed come up had now sat with the first gentleman, turned around and put his hand on my knee and said "Shhhh son, watch the game. I know it isn't the greatest team playing, but it's one in the making."

I turned to my father with what he described as a confused look, and my father said "You know who that is?"

I replied "No, who?"

My father said "Brian Clough. You listen to him, do as he says, and you'll be fine. You never know, you may end up playing for him"

Looking back, it's one of the fondest memories of my childhood. From that day forward, I concentrated on playing and tried my hardest on the pitch. I never became a professional, but I helped my local youth team, Meadows Colts, win the league and to the final of the Shield (the actual name of the Shield escapes me now).

I cried the day Brian Clough died, he really was an inspiration and a personal hero.

Clive Thompson

BACK IN THE LATE 80s my brother would've been 9 or 10 years old, and was planning a birthday party. Being an obsessive Forest fan he'd written a letter to Brian Clough to invite him for his birthday tea, rather naively and sweetly. My parents did their best to strike a balance between humouring his desperate desire that Mr Clough would indeed make an appearance along with preparing him for disappointment by pointing out how busy he'd be near the start of a season (his birthday is in October). Being a slightly less sensitive slightly older sibling, I constantly suggested a silver Mercedes had just pulled up outside, which naturally got him rather excited the first couple of times before he got wise to my cruel ruse.

Unsurprisingly Richard's birthday tea took place without an appearance from Brian Clough and despite having his friends and family in attendance he was pretty glum about it, but as kids do bounced back into regular life. A few days later a parcel arrived in the post addressed to Richard - enclosed was a football signed by the Nottingham Forest squad and a letter signed by Brian Clough thanking him sincerely for his invitation - and expressing his regret at not being able to make it round for his birthday tea - which naturally he hoped was enjoyable even without his company. I believe Rich still has the letter from Brian. What a spectacularly thoughtful gesture from a man who must've been awash with similar letters from supporters.

Rich went on to become one of the committee members who were instrumental in raising Nottingham's statue of Brian Clough, so clearly this exchange in addition to Brian's phenomenal influence during his formative years as a Forest supporter were things that struck a chord with him throughout childhood and right into adulthood. We are both now incredibly proud to see the statue in pride of place, and generally use it as a meeting place if we're getting together in Nottingham for any reason.

Rich did have the opportunity to meet Clough once at a book signing at the City Ground. Like any awe-struck young man he politely greeted the great man and requested to have his book signed. Predictably, perhaps, and not for the first time – Mr Clough instructed him to 'get a bloody haircut, young man'!

Tony Drake

SENT OFF

I T WASN'T THAT LONG after Brian had arrived at the City Ground and he had installed his famous "shed" dug out squarely on the halfway line. My mate Terry and I watched the first team playing stood on the Kop (now of course the covered and seated Bridgford End).

At the end of the first team match, two local school teams were contesting their cup final and anyone that wanted to stay on and watch this kids match was free to do so. Terry and I decided to stay and being in the days prior to perimeter fencing, we chose to jump over the low wall in front of the Kop and wander round to the Trent End. As we ambled round, of course, we came across the dugout shed and thought it would be fun to try out the best seat in the house.

My mate Terry did a wicked Clough impersonation and took it upon himself to become the Great Man himself. Shouts of "Now then young man" and "Take your hand out of your pockets" rang out from the dugout, whilst I just sat there having hysterics. Suddenly, with no warning whatsoever, BC himself appeared, from the side of the shed, clad in his traditional green tracksuit top, and boomed at us "Oi you two – fuck off!" Needless to say, we didn't need a second invitation and we certainly weren't going to stop and argue and we did exactly that – we fucked off!

Paul Bentley

DURING THE MID-1980's I played cricket for Sawley Cricket Club and on this particular Saturday we were playing at Quarndon where, at the time, Mr Clough lived. I was fielding out on the boundary when a Labrador/Retriever dog ran onto the pitch and its owner (Brian Clough) called and called for the dog to come back, which the dog totally ignored as it was having a great time running about on the pitch. Eventually, I managed to grab the dog and take it back to Mr Clough, who said in his usual manner, "Thank you, young man".

The game progressed and I was still fielding on the boundary when a ball came whizzing over for a four which I had no chance of stopping. It went over the boundary where Mr Clough was standing and he stopped the ball with his foot, saving me having to run after it. I went over to retrieve the ball and said "Thank you Mr Clough, saved me some running about." To which he replied with a slight smile, "OK young man, one good turn deserves another."

Michael Reeman

IN THE SUMMER OF 1967, which was Brian's first season with Derby, I was working for British Rail Carriage and wagon, as a machinist. Brian had been invited to make the Apprentice of the Year presentation, which always took place at lunchtime in the works canteen. As was customary for us, because we felt that it imposed on our leisure time, we carried on with our usual card school. This was not to last very long, as we were not prepared for Mr Clough. He noticed our lack of interest and at once addressed us as follows…

"Excuse me the four young men playing solo, I have given up my valuable time today to make this award. I do not think it would be too much to ask for you to give up a little bit of yours to listen to me." To our great embarrassment he then carried on with his speech and finally made the presentation.

It was then customary for the presentation party to be ushered off to waiting cars to be taken to the C & W Club for lunch but the organisers had also not reckoned on the fact that this was Brian Clough. Instead of going to the car he walked down the canteen pulled up a chair, poured himself a mug of tea and sat talking to us until the siren went to end our lunch break.

I must add that everything he said he was going to achieve at Derby County he did, and more besides. My only regret over this story is that he left us and achieved even more for our sworn enemies!

Mike Connolly

I WORK AT THE ROYAL DERBY HOSPITAL which used to be Derby City General. I now work as a linen assistant but when I started in 2001 I was a general porter. In 2004 I was working on the medical assessment unit (MAU) at the Royal. I was asked by the sister to transfer a "special" patient who had been admitted into the hospital the night before. When I entered the Private side room I was confronted with a male patient whose identity had to remain top secret. He had been admitted under his consultant's name and he was wrapped in blankets. It kind of looked like E.T. He was already in the wheelchair with practically all the ward staff hovering around him trying to get an autograph. I knew that the person in question was famous but as mentioned, he was covered head to foot in blankets.

I got the patient's property together to transport him to ward 30. As soon as we left the room the patient removed the blanket from his top half and the first thing I noticed was the green sweater. I instantly recognised him, I was speechless, it was Brian Clough! He started to talk to me on the way to ward 30.

"Do you play football young man" He said.

"No Mr Clough," I replied, "I have two left feet"

"Well" continued Clough "you can still play left wing!"

As we approached Ward 30 another porter was taking another patient from Ward 31 to x-ray. The other patient must of been mid 70's. Anyway Brian said to this chap "I want you fit for next season" and the old gentleman's face lit up. Brian had that aura about him. As we got to Ward 30 I entered the room in which Brian was staying and we were greeted by Barbara (Brian's wife) and as I was about to leave Brian thanked me for a smooth transfer and treating him like an ordinary patient I said, "No problem Mr Clough" (I was taught to respect your elders) Brain said "Call me Brian".

The only regret I have was I did not ask for his autograph (maybe I will get Nigel's).

James Hodgkinson

THE DAY I MET BRIAN I was at work at Derby Royal hospital where I work as a domestic. I was on a ward and went into a side room to empty the bin, knocked on the door and heard a 'come in' and as I entered I realised it was Brian Clough. As I bent down to empty the bin I wondered if I should say something when a voice said "and what's your name young man" to which I replied "It's John" and then he introduced himself and his wife and son to me. He asked me about my job and what time I started and finished. The next night I did the toilet bin next to Brian's while my work colleague went into his room and I heard Brian say "Hello John" then he said "oh you're not John" and my work colleague said "he's in the next room do you want to see him?" to which he replied "yes" so I went to see him and we talked about football. It was the same again and happened the next night as well, it's something I will always remember.

John Barton

I'M OLD ENOUGH TO REMEMBER BRIAN and have seen his sides play. I've been a season ticket holder at DCFC since the late seventies. When I was blessed with two daughters in the 80's I introduced them both to football. The elder one had a season ticket with me while Jim Smith was in charge; the younger one was too young to take to Pride Park. So after being invited by a family member I started watching Burton Albion (and DCFC) in about 1998 and took my youngest daughter with me to get her used to football thinking that one day she'd accompany me to Pride Park as well! Well she got hooked on the Brewers. She stood behind the goal at Eton Park close enough to touch the players and bought her own chips at half time with her pocket money! She absolutely loved it and we've both followed Burton ever since. Just like football should be!

As she got older she began to realise who Nigel Clough was, and to get to the story, who his father was! I promised her that one day I'd introduce her to my hero. So on Saturday 23rd February 2002 Burton played Woking in the Unibond League and as I walked round from behind the home goal at Eton Park with my daughter into the stand, we heard Brian before we saw him! He was holding court talking about the game surrounded by admirers and grandchildren! We walked slowly towards him and waited patiently while he finished his conversation. He turned around and with a lovely smile on his face said 'hello my lovely what can I do for you?' My daughter asked if Brian could sign her programme which he did, he asked if we were enjoying the game whilst signing my Derby Legends book. I thanked him for all he had achieved at Derby and then we returned to our place in the crowd. I said to my daughter 'one day you'll understand what that 30 seconds means to your Dad. The man who's just signed your programme is the greatest Football Manager who ever lived. A football genius in a world of 'flash in the pans!"

As you can imagine we've told and retold that story whenever Brain's name comes up.

Pete Smurt

LIFT HOME

WHEN I WAS IN MY TEENS in the late 1980's I was an avid collector of autographs of the Forest players and officials. One evening I was at a reserve team game and, after the match, I went to the players' entrance to see if I could get any more signatures. After the players left I decided to stay a little longer to see if I could catch Brian Clough. Ron Fenton, his assistant, was leaving and he asked why I was waiting. I told him I would like to see "the Gaffer". He said that he would be out shortly. When Brian appeared I asked him for his autograph and he did no more than to take me back into his office where he signed my book and we had a short chat about his intended signing of Lee Chapman (which happened a couple of days later).

When we finished he asked me how far I had to go to get home and said that he would get someone to give me a lift. When I declined, as it was only a short bus journey, he then offered to give me my bus fare.

At the end of a busy day how many other football managers would have taken the time and trouble to do what Brian Clough did on that evening? I will always remember him for his patience and friendliness.

Lisa Shirley

I MOVED TO SINFIN IN FEBRUARY 1971 when Derby County still trained on the pitch between the County Hotel and The Sinfin (Cock and Bull). I only remember seeing them training there once and recall Brian Clough calling out instructions and orders. I was riding around the pitch on my bike in awe of Hector, Hinton, Les Green and the rest of my footy heroes when I ran into Mr Clough. He semi-clipped me round the ear and said something along the lines of 'Watch it, sonny'. I felt as proud as punch that Cloughie, the boss of my team, had brushed his hand over my ear.

I often recall that moment when I pass the industrial estate that is now sited where the training pitch once was.

Mark Thompson

I HAVE ONLY MET MR CLOUGH close up on two occasions, once when I was 15 at the City Ground as a junior red. Mr Clough came into the Jubilee Club to answer questions, just being in the same room was so special and everyone were so nervous to talk, Peter Shilton was in the room at the same time signing autographs and this little lad said "Mr Clough what happened to Peter Shilton on Saturday" to which Mr Clough said "what do you mean?" he replied "he let a goal in Mr Clough". The great man replied "what do you want me to tell you young man? Tell him off" and the lad said "yes" after which he asked for Peter's excuse!

Steve Bent

KING OF EGYPT

FROM 1978-84 AND 1986-89 I lived and worked in Egypt. I was based in Cairo but spent time at various desert locations. Most years cigarette manufacturers sponsored European teams to visit Egypt to play 'Exhibition' matches against the National team and prominent local clubs in Cairo and Alexandria. In November 1979 Forest came out and whereas most Egyptian football fans had heard of and seen on television Manchester United, Liverpool, I spent a lot of time trying to explain the ins and outs of Nottingham Forest – then European Champions.

Anyway, the team and officials stayed at the Shepherd's Hotel in Cairo so, as probably the only expatriate from Nottingham, I called in on spec to welcome the players and Brian Clough to Egypt. On meeting Brian in the hotel lobby I admitted up front to being a Notts County supporter and his response was "Well, nobody's perfect, would you like to come to the official reception with us?" I didn't need asking twice so I climbed aboard the bus and sat behind Brian and Nigel Clough for the short ride to the Meridien Hotel where a buffet had between laid on and the National Press and television were doing their thing. I stood in the background with Jimmy Gordon. He gave me a signed photograph of Brian to mark the occasion and when it was the latter's turn to say a few words he said something to the effect, "Thank you for the welcome, it's nice to be here and we look forward to thrashing your national team tomorrow".

This first game took place in the 120,000 seater stadium in the Cairo suburb of Nasr City – adjacent to where President Sadat would later be assassinated on 6th October 1981.

By halftime Forest had strolled into a 3-0 lead and there was no way Egypt would score without a little help so the Egyptian referee gave the locals a very dubious penalty a few minutes from the end of the match and they scored to make the final tally 3-1. Now, Egyptian fans don't mind their team being beaten by a better side but they lose face in such blatant circumstances – and all this was on television. Shouts of "Coursa, Coursa" (Arabic for 'cheat') went up against the referee and at such times its tradition to try to set fire to the stadium. I was sitting in the lower tier and flaming newspapers and planks of wood were raining down from the tier above –

most of which created bonfires in the dry moat between the stands and the pitch.

We survived but the referee had to be escorted from the pitch under an umbrella of Police riot shields.

These events are 'normal' – the visits of Everton and Southampton were also very "interesting" – but that's another story!

Jim Pride

L ATE IN THE 1970'S I was a Police Sergeant on the Meadows at Station Street, Nottingham. Around that time I had to attend the Midland Railway Station to await the Nottingham Forest Football team returning from a European cup match. They were late and it was 1.30am when they finally arrived and the manager ushered a weary looking team on to their awaiting coach. Although ready to go, Brian Clough came back to the door and said "Thank you Sergeant for waiting for us. Good night" (a little means a lot).

My other wonderful recollection was at the Trent Bridge Cricket Ground around the same time, where I was a spectator. Brian also loved his cricket and on this day he was sat at the rear of the Parr Stand, with half a gale blowing and sparsely attended by the public. A boy of around 12 discarded a plastic cup which he kicked, left on the floor and started walking away. There was an amount of litter blowing around from a bin which had been blown over. Immediately a voice boomed "I say, young man, pick that cup up and while you at it you can pick up the rest as well."

To demonstrate the will power of the man, the boy sheepishly obeyed.

Mike Newman

STARSTRUCK

I MET BRIAN THROUGH MY SISTER back in 1983. My sister Patricia was out with friends at Blotts nightclub I believe, and Duncan Norvelle, the comedian, was doing a show there. My sister's friend was called over to a table in which Brian Clough was sat along with another man I was told was Alan Hill.

Apparently he said to my sister's friend he wanted to dance with my sister after having seen her dancing. My sister thought she knew his name but wasn't really into football but was none the less surprised to be asked to dance by the great man himself.

My sister mentioned to Brian Clough that I was a big Forest fan/supporter, and on this information he offered her two complimentary tickets to a match. When my sister told me about this the next day I was obviously surprised and excited at the news that she had met Brian Clough and that he had given two tickets to her for a Forest home match which turned out to be against Leicester City that Sunday (this was one of the first Sunday matches to take place) on 4th December 1983.

The tickets were VIP which included complimentary parking in the Main Stand car park. The best was yet to come as we were going to meet Brian Clough prior to the start of the match. We were both invited into his office where he stood up from behind his desk and greeted us both. Ron Fenton his then assistant was also present. I can remember hearing the crowd chanting outside and finding it hard to believe I was actually in Brian Clough's office on a match day.

We sat down and one of the first things he said to me was a bit of a shock when he said 'what are you doing with earrings in young man you're not a bloody girl' in a manner that wasn't offensive. After that he asked me what I was doing work wise and explained I had been recovering from a head injury caused by a car incident. In truth I was lucky to be alive - a van had tried to overtake an articulated lorry and the wing mirror struck me on the side of the head as I was standing on the kerb waiting to cross the road on Castle Boulevard. The hit to the side of the head was an eighth of an inch from my temple and had I been hit there I wouldn't be typing this now, nor indeed would I have got to meet the great man himself but enough about the accident.

He chatted away to us both which was only probably minutes but being in awe of him made it seem longer. He offered us both a drink and then said he would have taken me to meet the players but he hadn't got time and had to leave to go to the dressing room as the match was due to start shortly. In all of this I never asked for his autograph or a photo which I now regret but I was in too much awe to really think of asking to be honest. He wished us both well and left to meet up with the team in the dressing room.

On taking our seats we were sat next to our GP, the late Dr Ian Loch, who was then on the committee or at least had been on the committee. He mentioned he was present at the birth of Viv Anderson, known of course as 'spider' and made a wise crack about his long legs. at half time we went to the VIP lounge for sandwiches which were laid on and a drink and in there was the legendary Bobby Charlton, Ron Atkinson who of course many moons later was to take temporary charge of Forest and the late Dave Sexton former England under-21 manager and Man United manager. Also present I remember was a young Nigel Clough and Brian's brother I think his name was Barry?

After that match, which was a 3-2 win for Forest, Brian Clough kindly gave us tickets to a further couple of matches, though not in the VIP area which showed the generosity of the man. Having met him that day, he left a great lasting impression - my friends wouldn't believe I had been invited along with my sister to a match by Brian Clough and that we had been invited into his office on match day prior to a match. It was a good season in many respects as we finished third but sadly we were robbed of a place in the UEFA Cup final after match fixing by the ref and chairman of Anderlecht - of course that was leaked years later.

I never did get to meet him again after that but what a priceless memory, of the genius that was Brian Clough.

Roger Malbone

FOR MANY YEARS I WORKED in a newsagents on Central Avenue in West Bridgford. It was owned by Mr and Mrs Frank Allcock, then Stuart Dryden, who for many years was a very close friend of Brian Clough.

Back then the avenue was buzzing because there was talk that Simon Clough, Brian Clough's son, was going to take over the management of the newsagents. Then low and behold, it was true, 'Mr Clough' was my boss.

He used to come into the shop every Sunday morning, to purchase soft drinks, sweets and chocolates for the Forest players. I must admit, every time he walked through the door my legs began to tremble but he was always a breath of fresh air when he entered and his presence was known by everyone in the shop at the time. His first words were - "Hello my darling, how are you today." If shelves were not stocked up, then he would wander in the back and pick up the relevant box and start filling the shelves. However, on a bad day, he would have both Simon and myself running around stacking shelves and getting his order ready for him, demanding it was done at once.

However, Brian was a wonderful gentleman – charismatic, a committed socialist, eccentric, outspoken and often controversial. Some people thought that he had an aggressive nature, he probably did, at times, but everyone does when the need arises, but overall he had a heart of gold. Brian was often in the shop when a disabled child came in to meet him and the warmth, love, affection and generosity was always overwhelming. The smiles on their faces when they left the shop were great to see and brought a tear to my eye.

Overall Brian was a brilliant football manager, simply the best but a true gentleman with a very big heart as well. I will always hold extremely happy and fond memories of Brian – a man to be admired. I know he wasn't awarded an honour but in my view he should have been made knighted and I don't know why he wasn't.

My honour to Brian would be to call him - Sir Brian Clough.

Ben Shirley

TRYING TO REMEMBER SPECIFIC PHRASES is very hard, but overall, he was a gentleman when speaking to me. One thing he did used to say though - "Good morning my darling, how are you today".

He always used to come into the shop dressed either in his navy blue tracksuit bottoms, white or green shirt and green jumper, or occasionally in white shorts and once he did come into the shop in his white shorts, a blue and white t-shirt and jumped in front of me and said "Anyone for tennis?"

Marjorie Lincoln

I HAVE SIX GRANDCHILDREN. This little story is of my 12 year old granddaughter Cassie. When she was 18 months old my wife and daughter were out shopping in West Bridgford, they had to go to the local newsagents where Brian was sitting talking to his brother. On seeing Cassie he picked her up and said "my word I bet you're dar-dar is proud of you" and to this day she is the only one to call me dar-dar every time I see her.

Thanks Brian.

Colin Hugh

LUNCH WITH THE TEAM

IN THE MID SEVENTIES I was a collector of autographs. I was in my teens then and I would often meet up on a Saturday at Derby train station, and would often go to Crewe to seek any team who travelling by rail that day, Crewe was a good spot as a lot of teams had to change there. Anyway during the winter, it would have been perhaps the 1976/77 season, we stayed put at Derby rail station, and waited with our books outside the Midland Hotel, this was often used by Derby for lunch before their home games.

Coming out of the hotel mid-morning about 11.30 in a hurry was a certain Mr Clough, we asked if we could have his signature (there were only two of us) he said he would be back a bit later and then he would sign. He did not let us down, a bit later on his return he duly signed a few times for us, and then rushed back into the Hotel.

A minute later a head popped outside the main hotel entrance again, it was Brian or Mr Clough as we addressed him. He said "Come in lads and have some lunch with the team" and he duly escorted us through the main entrance and reception and into the hotel. "These boys are with me, and are going to have lunch with the team", he told the officials. We got down to the restaurant and he called one or two players over and said "Look after these boys, they are sharing some lunch today with you lot". We sat down with not a murmur, we were both shell-shocked.

But after that day, which I will never ever forget, I hold Brian in the greatest esteem as not only a great football manager but a great human being.

Taylor Weston

BACK WHEN BRIAN CLOUGH was manager of Derby, my Grandmother (Elsie Smith) and my Dad (Dennis Smith) were out shopping in the Park Farm shopping centre in Allestree one Saturday morning. My dad was only 3 at the time so wasn't any great help with carrying the shopping bags back to their house which was a good 15 minute walk away. Just as my Grandmother (with my Dad in tow) has walked around a shop building to make it back to the main road, struggling with the shopping bags, Brian Clough walks around the corner. He offered to drive them both back to their house with the bags in the boot. Being a kind lady, my Grandmother politely refused and wished him good luck for the match later that day. With that Brian Clough takes the bags and says that he'll walk home with them carrying the bags.

So Brian Clough on a Saturday match day morning, carried my Grandmother's shopping bags back to her house a good 15 minutes, so 30 minutes there and back. I've been told that he often offered local shoppers free delivery of their shopping bags if they looked like they were struggling.

Lisa Turner

I'M A LIFELONG FOREST FAN, Dad took me down my first game when I was about 5 or 6. He also took me and my brother down to a charity cricket match at Trent Bridge in about 1984/85 ish. It was Forest v Notts County at cricket and it absolutely chucked it down. My old man gave me the programme and a pen and sent me off packing in the direction of the pavilion to go and get some autographs; I was about 8 or 9 years old at this time.

I toddled off and entered the pavilion, an impressive building in itself, I walked in and towards the bar area where all the players were mingling and drinking. On the walls there were bats signed by Bradman and other greats, signed photos of Larwood and Voce, Hadlee etc. It was like a museum of magical cricket memorabilia, just thinking about all the famous cricketers that had walked through there made me nervous enough. I then met Stuart Pearce and Neil Webb among others who all signed my programme, Pearce told me not to spill his pint while I held it so he could sign the programme. All of a sudden as I was about to leave I literally turned and almost bumped into the man himself, Cloughie. I could have pooped myself; I was so nervous yet also very excited. Sir Brian took my programme and pen, handed me his beer similarly to what Pearce had done and told me not to drink it! I was so made up that day and for years after that I had met Cloughie, there was a real aura around him even to a small kid I really felt lucky to have had his time if only for a minute.

Years later my old man went in to the newsagents in West Bridgford, Nottingham, which Simon Clough owned I think. Brian was sat on a stool at the side of the counter and he made my dad take a free ads car magazine thing simply because it was free. My dad said "no it's okay thanks" but Brian insisted saying "take it, it costs nowt." I met my dad that very evening in the pub before an England game I think it was, he gave me the magazine and I kept it with all my old programmes etc. It was touched by greatness just like I was that day in the pavilion at Trent Bridge.

Harry Bend

A PAIN IN SPAIN

I INDIRECTLY MET BRIAN IN MAY 1989 when I was on holiday in Cala Millor, Majorca with 3 mates; we were out there celebrating my birthday. I am a big Rams fan and one of my friends Tony is a Forest fan. Nottingham Forest always used to go to Cala Millor at the end of the season so we just happened to stumble across the whole of their management team and players as they relaxed after a long season.

We saw Brian taking a stroll along the beachfront with Alan Hill and Ron Fenton, and at the time I was wearing a Rams shirt and Tony had his replica Forest shirt on. As we walked towards Brian he shook his head and hid his eyes (in a jokey fashion) as we walked past.

Anyway the same afternoon we called into a cafe for a drink and noticed that Brian was sat across from us and he spotted us again. A few minutes later he sent Alan Hill across to say that Brian was really pleased that Derby and Forest fans were good mates.

Hill was really good company and we spent ten minutes chatting about our holiday, my birthday and football. He wished us a nice holiday and went to sit back with Brian. Two minutes later, Hill was back with 500 pesetas given to him by Brian Clough for a drink for us all for my birthday. It was a nice gesture but Brian never looked up from his newspaper, which was typical of the man.

As mentioned I am a big Rams fan but we ended up

meeting the whole Forest squad during that week and they were an absolute credit to the club, well behaved... and you could tell who their manager was!

Phil Gough

I WAS AGED 13 OR SO with my mate Ed at a bus stop on the A6 heading into Derby. Ed with black and White bobble cap on when a not so plush white van pulls up and the driver with kids in the back says "want a lift into town?"

It was Sir Brian himself though in those days we'd have just got in anyway. We explained we were off to the shops in Nottingham and he was entertaining all the way to Morledge.

As he dropped us off he left us with the sage counsel "I'd take that hat off after Long Eaton, lads".

Wayne Briton

I ONLY MET BRIAN ONCE, it was long after he had left Forest and I think had been ill for a while. I was living and working in London then and I had been told he was doing a book signing not far from where I worked in the city. He was late, at least 100 people queuing patiently for the great man.

Eventually he arrived, but what struck me was the concern for the people with him, an elderly couple, not sure who they were. First thing he asked for was a chair for them, then once they were happy he turned to the crowd and looked at the first people in the line and that Cloughie magical line came out to this guy in his 20s "young man get a haircut, and get your hands out your pocket" to which everyone just burst out laughing. Not one person there minded he was late, or waiting for him to sort his companions out.

It says something that in the middle of London, long after he was past his best, that people were queuing outside by the time I left, must have been at least 100 people there. I can't believe they were all Derby or Forest fans either, such was the high regard in which the great man was held.

Tony Bentley

LATE TRAIN

I'M A FOREST SEASON TICKET HOLDER and met Brian Clough about 30 years ago. I was about 14 years old at the time and my brother and I travelled to see Swansea v Forest at the old Vetch Field. We travelled with the Forest Supporters Club who would regularly put on a train to away games and it was called Forest Rail. On this particular occasion the Forest squad, including Brian Clough and Peter Taylor, travelled on the train to Swansea with the fans. It was a freezing winter's night and on the way back about half an hour into the journey the rail tracks froze over, we managed to get to the next station but the train soon came to a halt and broke down. This happened before mobile phones were around so everybody had to queue to use the two payphones at the train station. As we realised this was potentially going to be a very late night everyone was eager to phone home to let people know we were going to be very late home.

I stood in the very long queue and a guy about 6 foot 2 came along, pushed in and stood straight in front of me. Me being 5 foot nothing and only 14 I didn't dare say anything about him pushing in when all of a sudden a voice from behind me said "Excuse me young man but I think this young lady was before you" I turned round and Mr Clough was stood behind me in the queue, the guy looked at me then looked at Mr Clough and said "Yeah OK sorry" and walked to the back of the queue.

Mr Clough was worried that I was on my own but I told him my brother was waiting for me on the train. I thanked

Mr Clough, we had a bit of a chat about the day and how cold it was and he signed my programme. We got back to Nottingham at about 1.30 in the morning!! Mr Clough a true gentleman and a legend.

Clark Wesley

IT WAS DURING THE SEASON after the first play off defeat, so 2003 probably, I was around 14/15. Clough had attended a game, the exact one escapes me, and was outside his son's shop. I went over and asked for his autograph, I'm sure he's had that request thousands of times but he waved me away, much to my disappointment. At this point a group of men across the road (I think they were sat in a bar) started pointing and laughing at me while I stood there on my own, programme and pen in hand.

Clough, seeing that I was being laughed at from the situation he had caused, turned around in a flash, put his arm around me, stuck two fingers up at the blokes, took me into the shop and gave me an autograph and a chat about me "staying good".

Jimmy Backer

THE HOT SEAT

THE FIRST TIME I MET MR CLOUGH would have been the end of early May 1989. It must have been half-term or something as I was a young 12 year-old at the time and had gone down to the training ground to watch Forest train. The training really passed me by to be honest, and no sooner had it finished than the players were packing up to head back up Trentside to the ground to get changed when I thought I'd go and wait outside the players entrance at the back of the Main Stand to get autographs. Forest were my club, and as an impressionable 12 year-old getting the chance to meet my heroes was just amazing; Stuart Pearce, Des Walker, Steve Hodge, Neil Webb, Steve Sutton, Brian Laws, Garry Parker, Lee Chapman, Nigel Clough (the player, *not* the manager!) - the list goes on and I digress but after the players had signed my autograph book, and headed off in their cars, which in those days normally had the name of the garage they'd got them from as part of a sponsorship deal, then I was getting ready to go home, when a certain gentleman in a recognisable green jumper and a flat cap came walking out of the entrance.

"'Mr Clough", I asked rather sheepishly, "can I have you autograph please?"

"Young man" was the immediate response, "follow me". Well, the next 10 minutes or so flashed by, they were a blur then, and even more of a blur now! Brian got in to his car, which was parked in the player's car park, a silver car if memory serves me correctly, maybe a Mercedes? He'd got in his car after asking me to follow him, but you tend to do what he asks, especially at that age, and I chased his car in to the main car park in the Main Stand, where he promptly stopped, got out and beckoned me towards the reception doors, which he kindly held open for me whilst I hastily made my way towards him.

Well, the next thing I knew I was sat in his office, at his desk, opposite the man who had taken my football club, my Nottingham Forest, to heights that frankly, look like never being repeated. My memories of his office however are clear;

clutter free, a cabinet on the left hand side of the office, and in the cabinet were no end of oversized whisky bottles, all unopened and all with 'Bells' on the front, so they must have been his many Manager of the Month awards he had gained whilst at the City Ground, and in front of me was the team sheet for the shortly to be re-played 1989 FA Cup Semi Final at Old Trafford, which would have been a matter of days later.

Brian asked me my name, asked me if I watched Forest, and which school I went to, and promptly gave me a signed photo, with those famous words on "Be Good, Love Brian Clough" that was how he signed most things in those days wasn't it? He thanked me for being so polite before sending me on my way. I was shaking as I walked through the Main Stand car-park and out of the red gates, but my, what a memory, one I'll certainly never forget!

The second occasion I met Mr Clough, well, I wasn't sure what to say really? It was a Monday night, Forest were at Notts County for a testimonial for Notts County's Mick Walker, five days before the 1991 FA Cup Final. Me and a friend were walking over Trent Bridge, towards the City Ground, not sure where to maybe the club shop to get tickets… I can't remember, but over the other side of Trent Bridge, heading towards Meadow Lane I noticed a certain Brian Clough and Archie Gemmill, one of his coaching staff at the time. My friend was a little shy but wanted his autograph, now me being two-years older than our last meeting, and with a lot more bravado, took it upon myself to cross the road and ask Mr Clough on my friend's behalf.

"Excuse me Mr Clough, can I have your autograph please?" I said, to which I got the response "Young man, fuck off, I'm busy"!

Well, what could I say, probably the same thing that I tell folk now. Brian Clough once told me to fuck off. Bizarrely, I didn't take the insult personally, that was the effect Brian had on you, and even now I take it more as a compliment and an honour as strange as it sounds!

Looking back and this is my opinion of course, the great man had clearly started to go downhill in those two years between meetings, the drink had started to set in and it had an effect on the way he dealt with the public, or maybe he was just in a foul mood at the time. I'll never know.

Tim Tyne

I WAS LUCKY TO WITNESS the Rams finest footballing achievements throughout the seventies all made possible by the arrival of Cloughie! As a mad keen 12 year-old autograph collector, I was eagerly waiting to add the 'Clough' signature to my collection when he arrived at the Baseball Ground in June 1967.

Sure enough this statuesque, well-groomed man, eventually appeared and started sauntering towards the car park followed by myself and at least a dozen more autograph hunters eagerly clutching pens and papers.

The normal scenario would be that the 'target' was completely surrounded and then subjected to enthusiastic jostling, as several pens were thrust at him the same time. Hopefully you would succeed before the 'victim' had had enough and 'legged it' to their car. That would have been normal but it was soon clear that on this occasion we were dealing with somebody who was everything but 'normal'.

"Right you lot" came the shrill tones, "if you want my signature then you had better all line up by this wall," we all stopped our pushing and did as the voice commanded.

"Right you can have one signature each, but not if I don't get a please and a thank you!"

Sure enough we all waited in line and approached him

with "please can I have your autograph, and "thank you very much Mr Clough ". I believe somebody did dare to call him Brian, but was given a frosty stare and a cuff on the ear for not following his instructions.

I still have the signed photograph from that day in my scrap book and can't help but chuckle when I recollect what we did to obtain it.

'Cloughie' was certainly a one off in every sense of the word.

Sue Montgomery

"It's Mr Clough To You"

MY FIRST EXPERIENCE of Brian Clough was when my friend and I went down to the Baseball Ground to buy season tickets a few games into the 1967 season. Brian was actually serving in the ticket office and looked after us throughout, even accompanying us to the Normanton Stand where we selected our seats. I didn't miss a match there during his whole tenure as Rams manager.

In 1975 I started a local football team called SRL'75 in the Derby City Football League, and my next experience of Brian was when we played AC Hunters in the early 80's (1980 or 1981). AC Hunters was the team that both Nigel and Simon Clough played for and they beat us 2-1 with Nigel scoring both goals. I had run the line during the match, and after the final whistle as we were walking off the pitch I heard this voice shouting me, "Oi! Linesman!" The great Mr Clough was shouting to me. He strode over and told me I was the fairest lineman he had ever seen! He had probably forgotten that remark 12 months later because when we played AC Hunters the following season, I raised my flag for offside and he shouted across the pitch "you need bloody glasses linesman"!

I eventually became Chairman of the Derby City Football League, a position I still hold today. We hold our Awards Nights at the Derby Assembly Rooms each May, relying on football celebrities from Derby County to present the awards to the players. In 2003 we were very honoured that Brian came along to present the trophies and the experience standing alongside him on stage will live with me forever. Unknown to all of us, he was ill with the cancer which eventually took his life but he stood on stage for an hour, presenting about 900 trophies. The atmosphere was electric – the boys, aged between about 10 and 16 who collected their trophies from him, stared at him as if he was God (which of course he was!). None of them were even born until his management career finished. The managers who accompanied the boys on stage stated that they couldn't believe they were shaking the great man's hand. The whole experience sent shivers down my spine! The highlight of the hour, however, was when a boy from an Ilkeston team shook hands, took his trophy and said to Brian "cheers mate". Brian snatched the trophy back out of his hand and said "It's Mr Clough to you" before smiling and handing the trophy back.

The Derby City Football League was honoured that Brian subsequently agreed to become President, an office which he retained until his death in September 2004.

What wonderful, wonderful memories of a great man. I was privileged to be invited to Brian's memorial service at Pride Park Stadium and it almost seemed like he was having the final word with the thunder & lightning which was banging around the stadium during the very moving service.

Ron Tyne

I PLAYED FOR AC HUNTERS along with Nigel and Simon. I was the youngest player on the team and Brian would often come and watch us play down at Meadow Lane. Sometimes he would say very little but at others you could be on the wrong side of a rollicking in his usual way.

During one game the pitches were bone hard, too hard for a stud so I had to wear a pair of white Pumas. This was also the day after I had completed the Four Inns walk (45 miles with a full load in the Peak District) so I was fairly knackered as it was. After missing a cross from Tony Clough by trying to volley it rather than heading, it got Brian going. He yells out 'just because you have white shoes on doesn't mean you can play like Alan Hinton. Get em off'

But he was a funny one! I came back from college one weekend to watch Hunters play at the Racecourse. I was sporting two earrings. As Cloughie sees me he says 'no puff is watching my Nigel play get em out'. Now he was quite intimidating of course so I did the right thing and took them out. After the game he invited my mum and dad and me down to watch Forest play where we sat in his office and went to the dressing room just minutes before kick-off to see the players. Amazing stuff. But that was how he was - you could never read him for sure.

Wes Derry

43

A WARNING

E VEN FOR TWO STRAPPING COLLIERS, nerves started to jangle as the build-up to our second European Cup final was in progress. This was a bit of a momentous occasion; we had personal dealings with the man himself. We went along to see them play Mansfield Town in the County Cup Final and it was just blind fanaticism really, we couldn't get enough of the Reds at that moment. The Main Stand made a change for us in this game as the crowd would only be small. On the way up into the Main Stand entrance there were some frosted glass windows and as I turned to climber the steps with my plastic cup of scalding hot coffee, Cumbo, my pal, was leaning against the wall half way up the stair. I looked at him strangely and he gave me a come on nod. I got closer and he made put his fingers up to his lips and pointed to the slightly open window.

Then whispering he said, "You can smell the rubbing oils" and pointed upwardly, "hark that's Taylor talking" and we listened and got bits of Peter Taylor's pre-match talk. He was saying those Mansfield lads out there are out to get you and we must beat them or words to that effect.

The pair of us shrugged and agreed we didn't think it was that important so close to Madrid. Forest were doing their stuff and we went back outside for a cuppa at half-time. On the way up the steps we listened again, hoping to hear what was said at halftime. I was smoking at the time and leaned my shoulder as close to the wall as possible. Cumbo on the other hand decided to leap and grab the window sill and have a look inside. He scraped back down and said that someone is on the treatment bench and was about to scramble up for another look.

Quick as a flash, Cloughie's head appeared as he opened

the window wide and yelled, "CLEAR OFF OR I'LL HAVE YOU PUT OUT THE GROUND!"

We scarpered into the stand like two kids who had been caught scrumping, it was faster than ever we moved on the pitch playing for Annesley. Back in the stand we laughed about it with heads swivelling round in case he had come after us.

Gary Awe

MY BRIAN CLOUGH ENCOUNTER occurred unexpectedly on 19th April 1969. Derby County had run away with the Second Division Championship and this was the final match of the season, after which Dave Mackay would be presented with the trophy. The team served up a feast of goals with Durban helping himself to a hat-trick as the Rams rounded off the season with a 5-0 victory over Bristol City.

As usual, I'd watched the game from the Boys' Enclosure at the Normanton End. It was a fine day and after the lap of honour and the celebrations nobody wanted the party to end. I was in no hurry to leave and hung about outside the Baseball Ground soaking up the good vibes. I watched with interest as the autograph hunters waited patiently outside the players' entrance. I wasn't really into the autograph thing. However, a special souvenir programme had been printed for this game and on the back page there were pictures of all the first team squad. Green, Webster, Robson (pause), Durban, McFarland, Mackay (pause), Walker, Carlin, O'Hare, Hector, Hinton. It rolls off the tongue like a poem. I think we only used 13 or 14 players all season. The sub was generally Ritchie Barker and later ex-Forest striker Frank Wignall. Nowadays it's not unusual to play 14 players in one match.

The full time whistle had blown at about 4.40pm, as was usual and by now it was well after 5pm. Sudden cheers and scrambling among the young fans indicated that our heroes were starting to emerge from the players' entrance. My mind is a blank as to whether I joined in the autograph hunt for this one-off special occasion. I don't think I did but I would need to search through my archive of football programmes to confirm that. However, what happened a few minutes later will stay with me forever.

I was standing in the middle of the road at the junction near the Baseball Hotel, not far from the entrance to the A Stand. Who should be walking through the crowd? None other than the very man that had made this unbelievable day happen. Brian Clough. In no time at all, a stream of youngsters started following him, pied piper style, waving football programmes in his face. Voices rang out "Giz yer autograph Brian". Some brave souls even addressed him as "Cloughie". At that point he stopped and turned. As the begging continued, I politely asked "Please will you sign this Mr Clough". At that point he swung round in my direction and said "I beg your pardon?" I froze.

He looked straight at me and said "Young man, would you just repeat what you said for the benefit of all these other supporters". Confused, I repeated my request. Signing my programme Brian put his hand on my shoulder. "This is the type of supporter that I want to see at Derby County. He has good manners. Firstly he called me Mr Clough and secondly he said please".

As the penny dropped, the other supporters took the hint and all of a sudden all you could hear were the words "Giz yer autograph Please Mr Clough". I'm pretty sure he obliged but by this time I'd turned away, a shy 13 year-old suddenly feeling 6 foot tall.

Liz Bacs

LOST IN BRUGES

I'D ONLY EVER BEEN to one football match with my dad before he was killed in a mining accident in 1982. I don't remember that much of the game but I remember standing on the Trent End at the City ground and that Peter Shilton was in goal. Before that game I wouldn't have classed myself as a Nottingham Forest supporter, I was more interested in the exploits of Liverpool, who, for some reason always seemed to be on Match of Day. After that game things changed. I don't know if it was the sway of the crowd and the singing, the familiarity of the Nottinghamshire accent or just the fact that it was such an exciting event. My first live game, my first half time OXO, my first sniff of the paper of a match day programme all stick in my mind. That day I became a fan of Nottingham Forest, following the results in the *Football Post* and when I would listen to Radio Nottingham for the match day broadcasts.

Everyone in my family knew I was, like most kids of my age, nuts about football. I'd not been to another game since my dad died until one day my Granddad made a rare appearance at our house and asked me if I wanted to see Forest play. Not just any game though. He had a fascination with buying Mercedes Benz cars and would often go to Belgium or Germany and usually come back with another car, much to the chagrin of his wife. I remember we were sat in the kitchen, just after my birthday when he asked me if I wanted to go with him to Belgium to see Forest play

Club Brugge. The match was in five days and it would mean missing school but that was the least of my concerns. I'd never been away from home longer than a night, and I'd certainly never been to another country so whilst I was excited, I was also very nervous.

We set off on a sunny morning on 1st October 1984 and drove down to Felixstowe to catch the overnight ferry to Ostende. We'd be gone three days and I'd packed enough Cheese & Onion sandwiches and Salt n Vinegar crisps for the journey down and the crossing.

After a night spent above a bakery in Ostende we travelled by train to Bruges and spent the morning looking at a few cars, pricing up pipe tobacco and just meandering. My Granddad was convinced that the stadium was only a short distance from the city centre and so after lunch we set off. We followed the floodlights and arrived at a beaten up, derelict stadium that clearly wasn't the one we wanted. We finally asked for directions and established that the ground was still a few miles away. The journey took forever (or so it seemed when you are 11 years old) and when we got to the ground the ticket office wasn't open and no-one seemed to be around. Thinking that I wasn't going to get a ticket I remember being pretty annoyed with my Granddad for not paying to take the bus or a taxi. Standing there looking at the ground, seething on the outside and sulking on the inside I was beginning to think that the whole thing was a waste of time. We were miles away from the city centre, it would be getting dark in an hour or so and we had no way of getting tickets.

I was disturbed from my thoughts of woe by the sound of air brakes. Behind me, a bus was pulling up. Not just any bus but a Redfearn coaches bus with a little sign in the front window with a red tree and the words Nottingham Forest

Football Club emblazoned on it. "It's the Team bus, it's the Team bus" I yelledand dashed across towards it. I watched in complete awe as the door opened and out stepped some of the players; Steve Hodge, Steve Sutton, Trevor Christie, Paul Hart, Ian Bowyer, Peter Davenport and Johnny Metgod to name a few and I just stood there. I didn't have a clue what to say and they must have thought I was just some local kid. My granddad on the other hand was chatting to a couple of the coaching staff and waving his walking stick in an animated fashion, I wasn't listening to what he was saying as I was watching a dark blue car pull up behind the bus.

I walked through the crowd of players and found myself standing next to the car. I was admiring the badge, it was a Mercedes. The car door opened and out stepped Brian Clough. I froze. I was just running my hand along the side of car as he stepped out and when I saw him I thought he was going to clip me for touching his car. You know, you have one of those moments where the seconds tick by and no-one says anything? Well this was one of them. I stood there looking up at him and he was staring at me. Eventually I stuck out my hand and said "Ayup Mr. Clough". I think the local accent totally threw him, but he asked me what I was doing there. I remember telling him it was my first time abroad and my first away game and that I was from Mansfield, which made him laugh for some reason! I don't know why but then I told him about my Granddad getting the wrong stadium, being too cheap to take the bus here and that my mum would not be happy when I told her that we had got there too late to get tickets. He asked me who I thought would win and of course I said Forest, by three goals, which made him laugh, especially when I added that Trevor Christie would get a hat-trick.

We stood there for a few more minutes talking about football, I told him I played in goal, but that I wasn't very good. At that point my Granddad appeared smoking his pipe and telling me to stop bothering the man. Mr. Clough said it was fine and then berated my Granddad for not taking the bus and making me walk and for not getting the tickets earlier. I could have died; I could see that my granddad was not impressed with me by the increased rate of smoke from his pipe (always a sign of trouble!).

The players were disappearing at this point, and a few of the coaches were looking our way and shuffling their feet. Mr. Clough asked us to hang on and went over to the coaches, who were all shaking their heads and checking their pockets. He then went to the door in the stand where the players had gone a few minutes beforehand and disappeared inside.

A few seconds later he appeared at the door and shouted us over. "Follow me", he said. Down a dark corridor we went and then turned left into an office. There was no one there at the time so he asked us to wait. We waited for ages. In reality it was probably five minutes and I was a bit relieved when I heard footsteps and the rather loud Cloughie talking to someone. "Here they are", in stepped Brian Clough and a guy with a blazer with a Club Brugges badge on it. "You need tickets?" he said in a very thick accent and over he went to a desk and took a stack of tickets from a drawer and handed us one each.

My granddad took out his roll of Belgian money and went to pay but the man (who I later learned was the secretary of the club) waved him away "They are free, my compliments". My granddad's eyes almost popped out as this meant he could enjoy several more Belgian beers than he was expecting later that evening. "What do you say?" was his only response and a prod of the stick at my knee. I thanked him and stuck out my hand for him to shake. To this day I have no idea why I did that but it amused him. He shook my hand and then gave me an enamel badge with the letters FCB on it. They talked for a few more minutes whilst I admired my badge and studied my ticket. Then it was time to leave so we went back down the same corridor, to the same door. Outside there was a Taxi waiting to take us back to the city. Unbeknown to me the secretary had arranged it when he had heard that we had walked there and that the ticket office was closed, I suppose he felt bad because we had come out all that way. All I remember was my granddad acting like he had won the football pools.

As I was about to get in the taxi Mr Clough stuck out his hand and I walked over and shook it, I felt very grown up. He then reached down and took his Forest tie pin off his tie and handed it to me. "Look after that young man, and behave yourself for your grandfather, otherwise you'll have me to deal with".

Forest lost the game 1-0, with a goal in the 89th minute. I was gutted. What's strange though is I remember the game like it happened yesterday. The crowd was really loud. At some point a hat went around the away supporters to help the striking miners who had come along to the game – funny I remember that. A touching gesture when you consider that many of them were working and the tensions that must have been around, I suppose it just goes to show that football, at times, transcends events.

I still have the pin and even though I rarely use it, whenever I take it out it always reminds me of the day I met Brian Clough.

Phil Montgomery

I MET BRIAN CLOUGH in the late 1970s or early 80s whilst I was working as a security alarm installation engineer in Nottingham. My supervisor one day gave me this job to provide extra security to a system at a newsagents shop in West Bridgford in Nottingham. Now I was no great football fan, but everyone was aware of Brian Clough but I had no idea that his business interests included newsagents shops, anyway, I arrived at the premises and saw the shop manager and discussed the work to be carried out and he pointed out a very smartly dressed young man working at the rear of the shop (sorting out papers for delivery if I recall correctly), he asked if I was a football fan and when I said no he commented that I probably was not interested that the young man was Brian Clough's son, but that Cloughie believed that all his children should start from the bottom and not ride on their father's shoulders.

Anyway I commenced work around 2pm I was working at the front of the shop, fixing cables above the magazine rack whilst standing on a step ladder when I was suddenly aware of someone tugging at my trouser legs. So I glanced down and then back up and the penny dropped it was the man himself, Brian Clough. Rather nervously I descended the ladder, aware of what the papers made of his temperament and his so called ability to bawl people out.

He very politely asked me what I was doing and so I told him, we discussed it for a few minutes, and then he asked me if I had seen the weather outside (it had gone very, very black and was beginning to snow heavily), I told him yes, that it looked as if we were in for a good fall of snow, to which he answered, did I have bairns at home, to which I answered yes I had four, and I think that I gave their ages (whether he requested this information or not I cannot recall).

He then told me to gather up my tools and equipment

and get off home to my family as they had the greater need of me, before driving became a difficulty and the road became blocked and hazardous. I told him that I couldn't do that because I was paid up until 5pm, also that there was a set number of hours laid down for each job, Brian again told me to get off home as the future of any family relied upon the safety of the father of that family and that if anyone at our company said anything I was to refer them to Mr Clough via the newsagents and he would put them straight.

Fortunately the snow blew itself out overnight and so the roads were passable the next morning and on arrival at work my supervisor, an avid football and cricket fan, asked if had completed the newsagent's job and when I told him why I hadn't completed the job, there were no questions asked.

A sequel to this story is that the following summer whilst working on the security system at Nottinghamshire County Cricket Club I was in the car park gathering my tools and equipment and Brian Clough drove in to play his usual game of squash in the Notts facilities, he spotted me, came over and asked if I had got home safely that winters night and had my boss said anything about my going home early, I told him no, he then asked about the health of my family to which I replied something like, that they were all okay. He said take good care of them and wandered off for his squash game.

Another interesting story not directly related to Brian Clough, was that prior to the above events, one or two years, I was working for a Derby security company and was working on the security system on a large new build house on Duffield Bank just outside Derby. The property was in its final stages and I was working in there with plumbers, electricians and decorators. The house was being built for Dave Mackay who had taken over from Brian Clough; I never knew who owned the property. We were all sitting around having a tea break with the usual radio on, as in all building sites, when the news came on that Dave Mackay had just been sacked.

Alfie Barry

I PLAYED LOCAL FOOTBALL a few times we played Nigel Clough's team AC Hunters when he was a youngster, Brian was always there. On one occasion it occurred to me that Brian shouted all the time instructing Nigel's team.

My own response was to keep shouting at our own team partially to drown out Brian. Apparently after a while he asked one of our off field followers who I was and commented "he shouts more than me!"

We drew the game and in the changing room afterwards he came and patted me on the back and said "well played number 10" he never commented on the shouting though!

James Bateman

I HAD TWO SHORT CONVERSATIONS with Brian back in the late sixties:-

I was a Telegram Boy back in 1968 and I was asked on a regular basis if I wanted to work at the Baseball Ground on the night matches, I had to lie down on the grass next to the *Daily Mail* photographer or the guy from Raymond's and when he said 'go' I had to convey the photographs that he had taken down to the Derby Telephone Exchange so that they could be wired back to London for the morning edition.

At half-time I was allowed to go in the press room for refreshments. On one occasion I was returning back to the pitch side and turned a corner just outside the press room and bumped into someone. As I looked up I recognised the person as Brian Clough, he said to me "Where do you think you are going young man" I told him what my job was and he said "well you had better watch out for my lad Hinton because when he kicks a ball he kicks it hard."

On another occasion I was parked in a Royal Mail van on Kedleston Road pointing towards Derby and I noticed Brian Clough's car coming from Derby towards Quarndon he was in slow moving traffic as he became level with me he wound down his car window and said "hey young man, your van has a flat tyre" I looked and replied "it's okay Mr Clough it's because I have a lot of weight in the back", he replied "I don't care it's flat and drove off".

I was so proud on both occasions that he had taken the time to speak to me.

Andy Shipton

THE FIRST TIME I REMEMBER being in close proximity to Brian Clough was when he turned up to see his son Nigel play for my local team Heanor Town around 1983–84. He sat with his legs over the seat in front eating a cup of mushy peas, I don't remember anyone approaching him and I'm pretty sure he was with his assistant Ronnie Fenton.

In the mid 80's Brian had a white Mercedes and around 1.30–2pm on match days, it rolled into the main stand car park at the City Ground. He would get out right next to the main entrance (where his small statue is now) and generally ignore the clamour for autographs. I do however remember one particular day when an Oxford fan (the days opponents) shouted out "we've come all the way from Oxford today" to which Mr Clough replied "I personally don't think it's that far" followed by a deathly silence where nobody wanted to make the same mistake of saying something. Clough then walked through the main doors saying nothing else to anyone. As me and my brother stood there thinking that was an autograph opportunity missed, the doorman asked us along with some other people to step inside. Once inside we were told to form a queue in a corridor and wait our turn, then one at a time we were shown into the manager's office where he sat behind his desk with his glasses on.

"What's your name son?"

"Justin",

Be Good Justin, Brian Clough, he scribbled in my autograph book, a memento I will never part with.

In the late 80's my brother was playing for the local kids team on a pitch in Derby. There was a men's game on the next pitch which nobody took any notice of until someone started bellowing "hit him". There stood the great man watching his son Simon play. Once the kids game had finished he was surrounded by autograph hunters and he obliged signing anything put in front of him. I remember someone asking if he'd been in a certain bar in Cala Millor recently where the landlord had suggested Clough was a regular, "never go near the place" was his reply, that was the end of that conversation.

Another memory from a similar period was when I went to a reserve game at the City Ground, it soon became apparent that he was there, sat in the directors box shouting instructions. Mid-way through the game he appeared in the B Block of the main stand and told two lads in their late teens to leave the ground. He then took it upon himself to chaperone them not only out of the ground but out of the car park too. As I stood at the top of the stairs at the back of the main stand, I could see him shouting at these two lads from the gates where the souvenir shop is now.

I remember other brief encounters such as being stood outside Carrow Road in Norwich and seeing him marching the team down the road towards the ground. I'm not sure why that happened, maybe the bus broke down? I don't know.

I think the last time I saw him before his passing was in the Robin Hood suite before a match around the year 2000. He was sat behind a table signing his books under the supervision of Kenny Burns. A shadow of the great man he once was but still on form and ready to rip into anyone at the slightest opportunity.

He was an incredible person and just had an aura about him that is hard to explain, he made grown men stop in their tracks in complete awe of him. The magnitude of him was evidenced at the ceremony at Pride Park after his death in 2004.

I had successfully obtained a ticket for the funeral in a cathedral in Derby but due to the overwhelming demand, it was switched to Pride Park. Sat amongst such legends as Viv Anderson and John Robertson we listened to stories from Martin O'Neill, Geoff Boycott and his son Nigel while the rain tipped down. I remember Nigel saying something like "I bet he's up there now saying look at those silly buggers sat there in the rain" but sit in the rain we did and everyone there would have done much more than that to have him with us for a few more years.

Justin Heaton

FOREST'S GAIN WAS ENGLAND'S LOSS

I AM FORTUNATE ENOUGH to have been a young Derby fan when Sir Brian was manager of our team. In fact it was our greatest team. Cloughie didn't necessarily go out and try and sign the best players about, he signed the best players for the specific roles he need filling within the team.

When he signed Alan Hinton from local rivals Nottingham Forest, they laughed saying that we would want our money back. However, it was the Reds who got mugged when Brian went in for him. Hinton was naturally two footed and equally effective down either flank and his passes usually met the head of the striker. I think it was the success of this signing that was the final straw for Forest. From then on they refused to sell Derby any more players. Not that this was the end of his attempted raids on our near neighbours.

Clough was determined to get Ian Storey-Moore. I remember him being introduced to the Baseball Ground crowd as a new signing. Forest found some kind of loophole and the transfer was eventually cancelled. Storey-Moore eventually moved on to Manchester United before his career was cut short by injury.

That signing aside, Clough and Taylor got just about every player they wanted. Any kind of manager who can get players to chose Derby and Forest above other clubs before the trophies were won, speaks volumes for the respect in which he was held.

Roy McFarland, a scouser, was on Everton's shopping list, but Cloughie turned up on his doorstep to sign him before the Toffees had the chance. Stories of him sleeping in Archie Gemmill's spare room and refusing to leave without the Scotsman's signature proves what a determined manager he was. There are so many stories about the man and many books have been written. I've read them all and watched many films. You just can't get bored of them.

Cloughie was a regular on TV as a match summariser and had a regular spot on 'The Big Match'. In this role he was box office. He wasn't afraid to dish out criticism either. One famous incident was when he called Poland goalkeeper Jan Tomaszewski a clown! This was before the Polish keeper performed miracles in net for his country to knock England out of the World Cup qualifiers in 1973.

Even when Cloughie and Taylor ended up at our main rivals Nottingham Forest, I couldn't bring myself to wish failure on that club. As a life-time Derby County supporter, I had to applaud their European Cup wins. Why? Because it was Cloughie's team. I know for a fact that some fans jumped ship when he was appointed at the City Ground. Another thing that was typical Cloughie was his honesty.

He won far more trophies with Forest (he was cheated out of a European Cup win at Derby, when Juventus were said to have bribed the referee in the semi final), but he never ever lost his love for us!

A few years before he died he received the freedom of Derby. He had already been honoured by Nottingham but when our City did the same he said 'It was the icing on the cake'. He stated that Derby was the best job he ever had. This isn't meant as a pot shot at our rivals either. It's well known that he regretted leaving us and even admitted that that he was silly for doing so. His return was on the cards many times with Peter Taylor often leading the way in trying to get him back 'home' to Derby. It was never to be though. Brian would not return to the club unless Sam Longson left. However, the missing chapter in his life was nothing to do with Derby or Nottingham.

The biggest crime ever committed by the Football Association was not offering Cloughie the England job. He would have got us nearer to a World Cup than anyone since Alf Ramsey. He could have got far more out of the players. He would have chosen a team of players that could work together. Any manager who can turn players like Larry Lloyd, Kenny Burns and John Robertson into stars is something special. Those players were going nowhere fast until he and Taylor came into their lives.

Because of the pig-headed nature of the suits at Lancaster Gate who were reluctant to have a manager who spoke his mind, the fans were robbed of the greatest manager of the day managing the national team. Sure it would have reduced the size of the trophy cabinet at Forest but I am sure that national success would have had their fans forgiving him for leaving.

Brian Clough, the man who took two struggling second tier clubs to the very top of the English game! The Greatest ever! Fact!

Andrew Buckley-Taylor

FOLLOWING FOREST AT THE AGE OF 15 in 1977 was exciting; travelling away and visiting all those First Division grounds we had only seen on Star Soccer or Match of the Day. Supporters clubs sprang up from every small town or collection of villages, Forest fans from our village of Kegworth decided to explore the Castle Donnington branch, very much a Derby strong hold.

Cloughie had pledged to attend all Official Supporters Clubs with a personal Q and A session. Our venue arranged, catering sorted and tickets sold out we counted the days off to meet our hero. As the day drew closer we realised that our event had unfortunately clashed with his appointment at Lancaster Gate as England sought a replacement for Mr

Revie.

The official word from the club was that Brian would still be attending although perhaps a little late due to this appointment in London. A packed house waited in anticipation for his arrival, many doubtful that he would even make it. I had no doubt and soon after 9 pm straight from London he arrived, did a full Q and A session, had refreshments with us and signed autographs.

He was indeed a man of his word, and what an entertaining evening he provided.

Simon Robinson

MY DAD RUNS A MARCHING DISPLAY BAND in Derby and has been since 1979. The band was formed by him and my mum and a few of my aunties and uncles in a place called Borrowash which is where I grew up and my parents still live. There's a local football club in Borrowash called "Borrowash Victoria" well Nottingham Forest at the time were obviously held in high regard by the football world due to their success at the time and it was a coup by Borrowash Victoria to organise a friendly against Forest at their football ground in Spondon, the main aim of the friendly was to open a stand at the ground. The Forest team involved players such as Pearce, Walker, Clough junior and was managed by the main man – Brian Clough!

My story gets more interesting because my dad's band were asked by Borrowash Victoria to perform at the half time interval. As my dad was a huge Forest fan he jumped at the opportunity so come the night of the big match the match came to a halt at half time and my dad's band performed their set routine on the pitch whilst the players were in the dressing rooms. The time came for the second half and the players started to come out and the band were still performing on the pitch with my dad watching on. Brian Clough strolled over to my dad and asked "is this your band young man" to which my dad replied, in the hope he'd heap loads of praise and thanks towards the band "yes Brian it is my band" Brian then replied "well get them off the bloody pitch we've got a football match to play" in his humorous but serious way!.

My dad was in awe of meeting to and speaking with Brian and wasn't offended in the slightest as it was just how the great man was!

Simon Holbrook

IN 1984 I WAS WORKING as a salesman for an Insurance Company, I won't bore you with the details but this policy we sold was very, very popular amongst footballers. Anyway as it happened we did not have many of the Forest team on the books, so one day I went in there unannounced and parked myself in the Club house, grabbing players and talking them through the policy as they came and went. Anyway I'd gone through the policy with one young lad who when it came to sign just said "I'll have to ask me dad first" and off he went. Later I was speaking with Des Walker, who said "you know who that young lad was don't you, that's the gaffer's son Nigel".

Later that day I saw Cloughie striding across between the offices and the Main Stand and in my best impolite tone shouted out "Oi, Mr Clough" to which he replied "are you talking to me young man? What do you want?" I introduced myself and asked him if he's spoke to Nigel about the policy, to which he said no he hadn't but I had better explain it to him. I went through the details and he nodded his head approvingly and then said, "I'll send him out with a cheque straight away". He then said "I'll tell you something young man, if you could kick a ball as well as you can talk, I'd have you in a red jersey and on that park straight away" with that he turned and walked away, and my audience was over…

Steve Haberfield

I MET BRIAN IN ABOUT 1989. I was playing football for a football team run by a lady called Carol Parker who was Brian Clough's secretary at the time and I remember getting an ankle injury on the Sunday. Carol told me not to worry as she would get me in at Forest to see the physio.

I was on a couch having my ankle looked at and lying on the next couch was Des Walker when suddenly the door opened and this head poked around the door and this voice said "I don't want to see you two in here come Saturday now get fit", it was only Brian Clough who had no idea who I was but didn't want to see me in there Saturday!

Andy Houston

I USED TO WATCH BURTON AT ETON PARK when Nigel was player/manager. Me and my mates decide to sit in the stand and the ref made a few bad decisions so me being me I shouted out 'having a fucking laugh ref' to all my mates sitting there not saying a word. So I said what's up with you lot, they said Brian is there. I looked with a red face at him and he said, 'you tell him son'. After that I didn't say another thing till the end!

Andy Shipton

I MET BRIAN CLOUGH WAY BACK when I was a hairdresser in Derby, My employer made a film for the cinema for advertising his shops in Derby. Brian came with John McGovern, John O'Hare, Alan Hinton and quite a few others.

I managed to cut John McGovern's hair for the film, Brian

was watching all of the time, I only saw the film once at the Black Prince Cinema in now what was Duckworth Square, not long after that the cinema was demolished and the then Top Rank Bowling Alley was built.

Dave Burton

ON THE BENCH

LEICESTER CITY V. DERBY COUNTY at Filbert Street. It was August 21st 1971 and I had just turned 13. Back in those days you could walk clockwise from point 'A' back to point 'A' round the ground, no problem. If you were a kid you could stand anywhere you wanted. We didn't have a designated seat or even stand like we do now.

I decided that I wanted to sit next to Brian Clough so I made my way around the ground until I got to the dugout in which Cloughie was sitting. There he was alongside Peter Taylor and Roy McFarland with Alan Durban sat outside the dugout on a canteen type chair. As I recall Durban was in a suit and so was not the substitute. The game had started and was around ten minutes old. I built up the courage and then tentatively placed my right leg over the concrete wall of the dugout: Cloughie said nothing. It was painful what with all the tension running through my muscles I was frozen to the spot with a leg stuck cocked over a concrete wall while watching the match with one eye and watching for Cloughie's response with the other. He didn't bat a lid.

After around 20 minutes of the game I built the confidence to actually sit on the wall. Another 5 minutes and my right leg touched the floor of the dugout. I expected to be blasted and lambasted: Cloughie said nothing. The half time whistle blew and Clough perked up "Right I'm off for now so if you want to sit here you can, and if you are here when I get back I'll see you later". Unbelievable.

Just before the second half started the players ran out and Clough, Taylor and the subs got into the dugout (with me now in it). Cloughie never batted an eyelid and just sat next to me. I was awe struck. He never spoke with me at all but just let me sit there. Alan Durban turned around to Brian and said "who's your mate" in his deep Welsh accent. Brian was concentrating on the game though. He blurted out to Terry Hennessey who was kneeling in pain point at his achilles tendon "don't be such a bloody wuss". He was in agony but Cloughie forced him to carry on regardless. I remember thinking at the time that Hennessey looked genuinely in agony and could not for the life of me understand why McFarland was never put on in his place but it wasn't to be.

The game went on, the whistle went, we won 2-0 and Cloughie disappeared as quickly as he'd arrived. It was as if I had never been there to him but he knew that I was there and allowed me to stay without question. You see that was the man he was. Kindness to a fault but very unforgiving. You had to be there to understand that much, and I love him for that.

Paul Topliff

A PHENOMENAL STRIKER

FORMER STRIKER ALAN PEACOCK played alongside Brian Clough at Middlesbrough in 1958. "Brian was a phenomenal goal scorer and is still one of the best in the history of the club," said Peacock. "When we first met he was in the RAF and I was working in the steelworks. We only ever used to meet at games on Saturdays for the first four years. He always had something to say about someone and that caused a lot of arguments. He said what he thought and you either had to take it or stuff it but he was usually always right.

"When I moved to Plymouth, he was manager at Derby. I got an injury and the club decided it would be no good for me to carry on playing. One of our last matches was against Derby and Brian came up to me and said 'come and play for us'. I said 'I'm finished, I can hardly turn'. He said 'I don't want you to play up front, I want you to play at the back'.

"Of course I hadn't played that position for a long time. After I retired I realised I possibly had another couple of years in me. I often look back now and think he was right."

Stan Anderson, who has written about playing with Brian Clough in his book Captain of the North, first met the brash young striker at Sunderland.

"A lot classed him as arrogant," said Anderson, who was the club's captain. "But as you got to know him he was quite sensitive. One of his first matches for Sunderland was against Walsall, we got beat 4–3. He came into the dressing room and said 'if we'd had any sort of defence, we'd have won that match', which was true enough.

"But I said 'Brian, that's not the thing to say, we play as a team' – he took it, fair enough. His main interest was scoring goals and that was it. There was no point telling him he'd missed a chance, he'd focus on the ones he scored."

Anderson said they became friends after they stopped playing together and described how he was going through a difficult time when Clough called to console him. Clough invited his former captain to be his guest at a Derby County match, "I'd had enough of football but he said 'I won't take no for an answer' and put the phone down, that was Brian. I had a nice day with him."

A YOUNG JOHN MCGOVERN first met Clough at Hartlepools United (now Hartlepool United) and went on to serve him at Derby, Leeds and Forest.

"It was exceptionally easy working for him if you were 100% committed to being a decent footballer," said McGovern. He was one of the best managers the game has ever seen. The most flamboyant and outspoken and he was an inspiration. When I joined Hartlepool, every time I got the ball I used to try to run with it past other players. I wasn't very successful. One day at training, Brian told me to dribble a ball around a corner flag and back as fast as I could. He then told me to do it again without the ball. Then he asked 'which was easier?'

"I told him without the ball was easier and he replied 'well why don't you try passing it on Saturdays then?'. I learnt that from him at 16 and I remembered it until my 30s. I'll never forget it because I took everything he said to be the way you play. He knew I was enthusiastic and wanted to play football, I wanted to improve and win, and he knew I was committed.

"Sometimes he would tell me to get off the training field and not to do any more. I just wanted to perfect my game but he would tell me to rest. 'Save yourself for Saturday' he would say. He had that knack of saying the right things, in the right way. He was always right."

ROY McFARLAND SIGNED for Clough's Derby when he was still a teenager. Under him, he won a First Division title and his first England cap.

"I was there for every single moment of Brian and Peter's six years at Derby," said McFarland. "They felt it needed two people to run the club and they helped each other. When I signed for Derby, one of the first things Clough said to me was that I would be an international player within 12 months. This was the first time I had met him and I thought 'what is he talking about?'.

"I had only just moved there from Tranmere Rovers, a fourth division team and thought he was mad. Him and Peter told me about their vision at Derby. They said 'lots of things are going to change here and we want you to be a part of it'.

"But he was wrong! I got my first under-21 cap for England 14 months after signing. When I look back at it, and what they said, I realise they made it happen. There were no international players in his team when I joined but eventually every one of us was an international footballer. He was so confident and forthright in saying things. He would forecast things and say we would win the First Division, championship and we'd get promoted from the Second Division. Everything they said, all those predictions – they made it happen."

★

STEVE PIPER was one of Brighton's youngest players during Clough's brief time on the south coast.

"Brian liked the younger players. We were all in the early stages of our careers and were absolutely frightened to bits of him and did exactly what he wanted us to do," said Piper.

"I was only 20 at the time and played very well for him so it worked for me. We had a decent relationship. Once I got sent off in a game against Shrewsbury Town for kicking Alan Durban, who was their player-manager. I kicked him up the bum in a bit of a red mist moment and rightly so, I got sent off.

"Alan played under Brian at Derby County so they knew each other pretty well. They got together and travelled from Derby to London for the hearing with the league committee. The committee there must have been absolutely terrified of them because I got let off. Alan and Brian went out of their way to come and help a young lad they didn't really know and that is the sort of person that Brian was. I was very lucky that day."

PETER LORIMER played for a hugely successful Leeds United side under Don Revie but he said it was an unhappy time under Clough.

"On the first day in the job he told us we'd been successful but we'd not won anything fairly and we should throw all our medals in the bin," said Mr Lorimer. "That was his opening gambit."

He believed much of Clough's resentment came from his time at Derby County and coming off worse against Revie's Leeds. "He said I was always dramatic and that I dived for penalties. We'd worked so hard and for him to come in to say these things was professional suicide. I had nothing against Brian but he never gave himself a chance and without Peter Taylor he was a loose cannon."

Despite what happened at Leeds, Lorimer believes Clough should have been given the England job at the end of the 1970s. He also represented Leeds United at the memorial service for Clough at Pride Park in 2004.

STAN ANDERSON, who Clough had become good friends with after their time at Sunderland, was managing QPR when they beat Leeds in August 1974. It was a result that contributed to Clough's sacking at the club after just six league matches.

"I could see he was rather depressed and I said 'what's the matter, Brian?' and he said 'we've just lost the match'. I said 'look Brian, this is a top class club you've come to, you've come a long way since Hartlepool'." Clough was sacked a few weeks later but Leeds paid out on his contract, setting him up financially for life.

"He said to me 'I've earned more money getting the sack than I've done in the whole of my career.'"

JOURNALIST DAVE ARMITAGE first met Brian Clough in the mid-1980s when he started working for the *Daily Star*.

"Cloughie was pretty intimidating, even to the most seasoned campaigner but he was box office," said Mr Armitage.

The journalist, who has compiled three books of short stories about Clough, once bought the manager a present. He had visited Shrewsbury Flower Show and spotted a variety of sweet pea named after him. The young reporter bought a couple of packets of seeds and presented them to Clough the next time he interviewed him.

"He said 'are these what I think they are? Are they my sweet peas?'" Clough explained he had given a nurseryman permission to use his name after he had cultivated a new variety of the flower.

About a year later Clough shouted across to the reporter. "[Clough] said 'hey, my missus has grown those sweet peas and they're absolutely gorgeous'," said Mr Armitage. "She said I ought to invite you over to see them but I said I'm not having shithouse journalists at my house!'"

Mr Armitage said that was Clough's way and eventually he did get an invite to his home. "[The sweet pea gesture] meant something to him," he said.

NOTTINGHAM POST PHOTOGRAPHER TREVOR BARTLETT and reporter Duncan Hamilton became good friends with Brian Clough during his time at Forest.

"It took a while to get to know him. He could be a cantankerous old bugger at times," said Mr Bartlett. "He never liked managers and directors but he always had time for everybody else. Once we were at his house after a trip to Wembley and he took off his suit jacket, checked the pockets and said I could have it. It was a really nice thought. It just shows how unbelievable he was.

"I was absolutely chuffed. I put it on and went straight to my local pub to show it off. It was big on me and I didn't wear it again. I kept it in the wardrobe for about 10 years."

In 2011 Mr Bartlett donated the jacket to a charity auction at the City Hospital in Nottingham where it raised £1,000.

"I used to see him pretty much every day for the best part of 15 years," said Mr Hamilton. "In '82 at a Forest pre-season tour in the Netherlands, BC saw a tree he liked. But they were all travelling on the plane and me and Trevor were on the ferry, so he asked if we could bring the tree back for him.

"We were sweating all the way with it in the back of the car covered in coats, bags and anything we could find. I can't even remember what kind of tree it was but BC was exceptionally keen on his garden so he put it in there. It's probably still there."

MORE FANS BEHIND THE LEGEND

When I was about 7, I lived in Derby with my mum, and my dad lived in Leicester. I had been visiting my dad and he had taken me to Derby Train Station to go back to my mum, I was wearing my Leicester shirt and someone pulled my shirt slightly, I looked up and Brian Clough was standing above me smiling. My dad asked for an autograph, he agreed, What a Legend. This was in 2003.

Owen Wain

In December 1968, Brian Clough dressed up as Father Christmas and came to my nursery in Allestree, Derbyshire. I'm the girl in the photos. I believe he was manager of Derby County at the time and lived in the village.

Wendy Moore, Pointon, UK

He approached the Dell crowd at Southampton just before kick-off one night and I joked: "I hope your players have eaten their Shredded Wheat, they'll need it," in reference to a TV advert he had done.

He replied to me: "Now, young man. You'll be pleasantly surprised by what my team can do tonight." They walloped us!

Bill Kenchington, Southampton

I was a young sign writer in the late 1970s. I was sign writing a wall near Trent Bridge, about 500 yards from the City Ground, when Brian Clough walked past and stopped to watch me work for a couple of minutes. "Very skilful young man," he said. "Thank you sir," I replied. I hadn't called anyone sir since I left school. It just seemed the correct thing to say.

Gary Jarvis, Nottingham

I met Brian many years ago when he lived in Quarndon. As a police officer, I went to his house whenever his alarm went off. A lifelong Forest fan, I had a chance to talk about the European Cup final that I had been to. The conversation went. Me: "Do you know, Brian; I watched the last half of the match against Hamburg through my fingers as I couldn't bear to watch." He replied: "Do you know, son, so did I," and he smiled. He had the knack of making every person who met him feel special.

Philip Severn, Alfreton, England

As a 12-year-old boy, I went to watch a Nottinghamshire v Yorkshire cricket match. I got there early and a certain Mr Boycott asked me to do him a favour and "take two tickets to the gate for a Mr Clough". I met Mr Clough and his son, whereby he gave me £5 and asked me to sit with him and the Yorkshire and Notts teams of the day, have lunch and tea with them. I did the same thing three days on the bounce. Brian Clough, Eddie Hemmings, Geoff Boycott, Richard Hadlee, Tim Robinson, Chris Broad, David Bairstow. I've still got goose bumps now.

Andrew O'Sullivan, Worksop

I was driving on to the fly-over on Lenton Boulevard in Nottingham and the traffic was slow because a car had broken down and someone was helping to push it out of the way. I got out to help push and as I did, I noticed the bloke pushing next to me was Clough. I just couldn't say anything as I, like most in Nottingham, was in awe of the man. We got the car started, he said "thank you young man."

Jake Murray, London

When I was a kid, I used to hang around the car park on match day at Forest getting autographs, ran up to him one day and he duly obliged. But he then took me to one side and gave me stern warning. He said: "I'm watching you son and you better not nick anything."

Paul White, Nottingham

My father, Paul Barron, played in goal for QPR against Forest at the City Ground once. He walked off the pitch after a 0-0 draw and as he entered the changing room, somebody kicked him up the backside. He turned around to see Brian Clough, who said: "That'll teach you to keep a clean sheet against me young man."

Joe Barron, Nottingham

Brian was in the bar at the old Eton Park in Burton. My dad asked him about when he won the Championship with Derby and Brian came over to tell us the tale. He looked at me and said: "Young man, get me a chair." My dad offered him his own but Brian insisted "the young man will get me a chair". He told his story and left the bar to chants of "one Brian Clough" from the Burton fans.

Alex Winter, Wimbledon

My mother was a cleaner at Marton Grove School where Brian was head boy. He always had a kind word for her and she said on many occasions when walking by her as she moved from one room she'd hear his voice behind her as she prepared to move to the next room. "Hey boy, don't walk by it, pick up Mrs Appleby's bucket and carry it for her." Brian was very special to my mother.

Joe Appleby, Chattanooga, USA

He did a radio advert for me when I was at *Match Weekly*. We recorded it at Radio Trent and he said he must be back at the City Ground by 8pm to attend a board meeting. He only had one line listing all the stars contributing to the first issue. I knew his voice would be instantly recognisable on radio but he couldn't get it right. To my horror, I looked at my watch and it was 8.30! "Brian," I said, "it's 8.30 and you're late for the board."

"Bugger the board," he said, "we'll get this right first" – which he did eventually.

Mike Wells, Purley, England

BBC Radio 5 live's Pat Murphy memories of Brian Clough – "Cloughie was always very kind about the personal lives of those he allowed into his confidence. When he heard my mother was dying of cancer in the summer of 2004, he sent her flowers and a touching note."

In the early 80s, my mum worked at a residential home for adults with learning disabilities in Melton Mowbray. Everyone was Forest mad and the officer in charge wrote to Forest asking if the residents could go and watch the team train and possibly meet some of the players. The group were duly invited to the City Ground one morning and sat in the stands to watch that amazing team train and, as the players went back in to get changed, they waved at the group as they prepared to go home.

They assumed that was it but they were then invited into the players' lounge and the whole squad came in to meet them, and spent an hour signing autographs, talking about football and making their wildest dreams come true. They were elated. A great man, often abrasive! But with a heart of gold.

Alastair Hilton, Phnom Penh, Cambodia

Brian's penultimate game as boss was a County Cup match against Notts County, and I was chosen to be one of the ball boys. We were lined up in the tunnel before kick-off when Brian - in trademark green sweater - walked up, got down on his knees and said: "Come to granddad." All of us ball boys then gave him a hug in turn. It was a slightly comical situation, but I was almost in tears.

Woz, Nottingham

I used to work at The Royal School for the Deaf in Derby. During the early 1970s some of our members met with some minor hassles at a home match. Clough heard about this, and gave us a permanent free pass to attend all games at the old Baseball Ground.

Richard Morris, Mouthiers, France

I met Brian Clough and Peter Taylor in France in 1979. The day before, a group of French lads on our camp site told us that Forest were playing 20 miles away in Montpellier. Mr Clough had agreed to take the European champions to the south of France for a few days in the sun.

After the game we met Brian and his assistant, Peter Taylor. We wanted to talk about football but Brian was more concerned asking about the suitability of the nearby beaches for his family (including 13-year-old Nigel). Both Peter and Brian were so relaxed and down-to-earth and wished us well for the rest of our holiday.

Adrian Taylor, Canterbury

Aged seven, I sent Brian my autograph book by post. He sent it back to me signed: 'Dear Jonathan, Be good, Brian Clough.' I am 42 now and that one action made me a lifelong Forest fan. How many managers would do that these days?

Jonathan Clarke, Twickenham, UK

When I was 10, my parents took me to the City Ground to watch an open training session. I was in the Scouts at the time and we were doing a sponsored tea making. Afterwards, we were behind the main stand when Mr Clough came out. We were able to get his autograph but not content with that, my dad asked if I could make him a cup of tea. The great man did even better than that, he took me by the hand and marched me inside and introduced me to all the players. I can still see the shell-shocked look on my parents' faces when Mr Clough finally returned me to them.

Stephen, Nashville, USA

The first time I met Sir Brian Clough was in 1977. We'd just got promoted back to the old Division One. He told me to buy a season ticket if I wanted to see all the games because most would be a sell out. So I bought my first season ticket and he said 'I'll bring back the good times'. How true he was.

Andy Linley

I remember being at secondary school back in the early 1980's (Grove Comprehensive, Balderton, near Newark) and Brian was the guest speaker at the end of year 'Speech Day'. The quote I will always remember is when he said: '...and when your teachers tell you that it's not about the winning, it's the taking part that matters, well, that's rubbish. Of course winning matters. That's why we keep score.'

I use this quote myself, even now, when encouraging my daughter in her sports.

Mark Milford, Grantham, Lincolnshire.

I used to sell scratch cards for Nottingham Forest in the 1970's and was in the Pools office at the City Ground the day Mr Clough was being shown around by a club official. It was in the first month of his arrival at the club and I was about 24 years old. As I stood in the office, Mr Clough's voice rang out: "What do you here, lad?" "I sell scratch cards," I meekly replied. Mr Clough said to the Forest man: "It's men like this that keep this club going." From then on, Mr Clough could do no wrong in my mind.

Geoff Williams.

I never met him, but like the Beatles, Bill Shankly, George Best and precious few others, he brought a ray of sunshine into my northern childhood. I used to live in Manchester. I remember when Forest were riding high and Cloughie was the man we City fans loved to hate. They came to Maine Road and we beat them 1-0 with a goal by the legendary Pole, Kazu Deyna. What I admired about Clough was the way his teams played and his ability to bounce back. I also remember him on the soccer panels on TV – he was a breath of fresh air. He christened the '74 Polish goal keeper a clown and showed no sympathy for the Brazilian keeper when Francis Lee kicked him in the head in a 50-50 situation, saying 'if you put your head in that way you can't complain if it gets kicked' or words to that effect.

Andrew Demetriou, Nicosia, Cyprus

Born and raised in Manchester, I am a life-long City fan. Around 1959, my father forced me to attend a league match at that place we don't like to mention! You know, just up the road from Old Trafford Cricket Ground. The Reds were hosting Middlesbrough and a home victory was inevitable. However, my eye was caught by the lively, classy and slightly arrogant Middlesbrough Number 9 – clearly a cut above the mediocrities with whom he was playing. Like all the other little kids, I was passed over the heads of the crowd to stand right at the front, directly behind the Stretford End goal. I still have this picture in my mind of him – ending up grabbing at the back of the net having gone up to challenge at a corner, no more than 10 feet away from me.

Some home fans might have wondered, 'Who does he think he is?' Brian Howard Clough, of course. Not necessarily the greatest human being in the history of British competitive sport… but in the top one!

Howard Paul, Chiang Mai, Thailand.

He should've been knighted when he was alive. Football is essentially an entertainment business and Cloughie was at least as entertaining as his teams and some of them won the European Cup and the League. If Fergie and Bobby Robson are 'Sirs', then it is only right that Cloughie joins them.

Karl Hoskin
(an Arsenal fan, who would have loved
Cloughie to manage the Gunners).

Brian was a lovely man. I worked with him on a TV commercials script for Parker Pens with the actor Arthur Lowe. It was shot in the boardroom at Arsenal, when Terry Neil was the Gunners manager. The press were tipped-off that Cloughie had been spotted at Arsenal and within half an hour there was a media scrum outside Highbury. Terry Neil had to come down and tell the assembled paparazzi that Cloughie was only doing a TV ad!

**David Horry, former advertising executive,
now living in Shanghai, China.**

Despite not being born until Cloughie's final season as a manager, I have grown to adore the man – and I am not a fan of Middlesbrough, Hartlepool, Derby or Forest. Clough was such a character with such a heart, and such an undying passion for the game. The greatest tribute I can give him is that, whenever I'm feeling down or in need of inspiration, I go through some of his old clips and videos, and I instantly feel better. I never met Brian, or even understood who he was until shortly before his death, but I feel like I know him. As Old Big 'Ead once said about his great friend Peter Taylor, I hope he's alright.

Greg Lea, London

I am the Portuguese director of the Russian online newspaper PRAVDA.Ru. I would just like to say that I remember Cloughie with many smiles and a great deal of respect. I am sure that this is how millions remember him. He brought to English and world football a special characteristic which was very much born with him - a wild flame, an unbridled horse, a raging fire. The boldness to try new ideas and the strength to keep to his convictions.

That is why he was so hugely successful - and we must remember he did not take over billionaire clubs with fat pay cheques, he made the clubs himself. Derby and Forest were nowhere when he brought them onto the map. He brought a lot of fun and joy to a lot of people for a lot of years. Thank you.

Timothy Hinchey

As a Gooner living in Peterborough in the 1980's I often used to watch Cloughie's Forest if I was not at an Arsenal game. Forest under Brian Clough played football how it should be played: entertaining, disciplined, tactics made simple and always easy on the eye. These were Cloughie's trademark for football during his 18 years at Forest.

There's only one Brian Clough (today's managers will be relieved at that!)... a football legend who would be successful in the Premiership even in today's game.

Keith Goulding

I only saw you once Brian – you were in your famous green sweatshirt alongside Peter and I was a young kid in the stands at Highfield Rd, Coventry. Although I was a mad CCFC supporter, you and your team were the example of 'magic' in football. Your genius was not lost on this young kid and I will always remember the 'Yarwood, follow that' line on the 'Whole World in His Hands' record – what superb comedy that was. Brian – you are missed. Love to your family.

Mark Pitt, Atlanta, USA.

I am a fan of English football, and wanted to give all respect to one of the greatest coaches in the world, Old Big 'Ead. Simply the best, Brian Clough. Thanks for what he gave to football. Greetings from Costa Rica.

Federico Carrera Rivas, San Jose, Costa Rica.

I'm a Sunderland fan and 14 years old. I think Brian Clough was a legend – the greatest player and manager there has ever been. Should have been England manager. Brought Derby and Forest from nothing to league champions. I can't think of any other manager who has done that. He should have been Sir Brian Clough. RIP Cloughie.

Joe Cox, Sunderland

Thank you for that great statue for a great man. He should have been knighted, he should have been England manager. I am a Man United fan – I live in Manchester, but my Dad and I were right behind his team in Europe all those years ago. Thank you, Brian, for the memories.

Tony Dunn, Manchester.

I'm Scottish and I'm 54 years of age. I never met Mr Clough but I feel like I grew up with him. He was always on the telly and seemed like a family friend, being in our living room so often, as a regular visitor to my home. One of my favourite stories about Brian is how on travelling on the team coach to Celtic Park, from Glasgow Airport, he spotted 'Davie Hay's' (the pub of the then Celtic manager) and ordered the bus to stop and all his staff went into the pub to enjoy some 'refreshment'.

They all had a drink at the expense of Davie Hay as, when Clough was asked to settle the bar bill, he told the barman to see 'the Celtic manager!' Nottingham Forest had their 'away goal' safely tucked away after that bit of psychology. Brilliant stuff from one of the true originals, and there weren't many, even then!

Keith Landles, Edinburgh

I would just like to extend my gratitude to you for honouring a legend like Mr Clough. I call him this because when I arrived at the City Ground for a trial aged 14 he insisted I address him as such – whereas my uncle Eddie was permitted to call him Brian. Although, I was only at your great club a short while, the man left his mark on me and I will never forget him. I have just recently got my coaching qualifications and it is principally down to Mr Clough's inspiration that I chose to go down this route.

It is shameful that English football as a whole doesn't give him his full credit but there are those of us who realize that some people are too important to be forgotten. I must point out at this juncture that I am a lifelong Liverpool fan and a proud Dubliner – but his effect on my life and my football thinking is a testimony to the power of this one off human being. With love, respect and gratitude.

Peter Smith, London

The best tribute I can pay Brian is that I witnessed his Nottingham Forest team come to Old Trafford on December 17th, 1977 and destroy Manchester United 0-4 in front of 54,000 people. I've seen teams win well at Old Trafford before, but no team has outclassed United so spectacularly in my time as a Reds fan. It was a pleasure to witness a team come and perform like that, even if the team I was supporting was on the receiving end. Brian was a complete one-off in terms of achievement, character and status. Of course, there have been other successful characters like him but none are loved and remembered as fondly as he is today. He is sorely missed as a person, and particularly in football.

Graham Wilde, Canada

I am a Celtic supporter, but I will always admire Brian Clough. He had huge success at Derby and also Nottingham Forest. He was the greatest manager England never had!

Michael Foxton

Brian Clough was and always will be my hero. I now live in New Zealand. My fondest memories are of Brian and the team showing the European Cup in the Market Square and Brian signing my Forest shirt. Still have the shirt. Long live Brian's memories.

Marco Baguley, New Zealand

I was never a soccer fan until Cloughie took over Nottingham Forest and then I was hooked with the success he brought to a minnow club. I will never forget their 2 European Cup triumphs and the accolades they achieved along the way. RIP Brian Clough. There will never be another manager like him, a once in a blue moon manager.

Noel Baldwin, Echuca, Australia

I've just read Cloughie's autobiography for the second time. A true legend and the most remarkable British football manager of all time. His family must be so proud that his legend lives on. I'm a Chelsea fan but can remember supporting his Forest teams in European competition when I was a lot younger. All the very best to Cloughie's family.

John Winning, Langley, Berkshire

I'm a lifelong Wednesdayite, and have been following them for over 35 years. That said, I've always believed that Mr Clough was indeed the greatest manager England never had. His death has been a tragic loss to football. I would whole-heartedly support any campaign to give him the honour he deserves.

Garry Lee Jackson

As a Bristol City supporter, my first match was against your Forest side in the 1989 League Cup semi-final when you got to Wembley. I have long since forgiven that result and the biggest complement I can pay you is that your achievements at Derby and Forest show that no matter how bad it gets, never give up hope. Dreams can come true. Wishing you all the best.

Jon Phipps, Bristol

He took two small town clubs with little financial backing and won two European Cups and two League Championships, and four League Cups, with stylish football.

Nick Parker, Nottinghamshire

I was doing the PA at Sunderland's Stadium of Light when Cloughie came onto the pitch. A colleague interviewed the Great Man pitchside. I was dead jealous until he asked Cloughie what he thought of the new stadium. Quick as a flash, in front of 42,000 people, the Great One spoke 'Young man, it's far better looking than you.' My pal dissolved as the crowd lapped it up. I'm now working in Dubai and want to thank you for keeping me in touch with the reality of life, namely football.

Steve Colman, Dubai

He feared no-one and had the balls to do the job. A real genius with a sharp tongue and even sharper mind.

Kevin Lockhart, Nottingham

He was the best because what you saw was what you got. Arrogance tempered by sincerity. Simplicity boosted by genius.

David Reeves, Derby

He was the greatest because he got the best out of so-so footballers and turned them into world beaters.

N. Kelly, Kent

Brian Clough was the greatest manager because he created something from nothing and that something was Nottingham Forest - the best football club of all time.

Jacqueline Gregg, Nottingham

I saw a brilliant interview with Brian Clough a few weeks ago on ITV2. The interviewer was Ron Atkinson. The funniest bit was when Brian was asked about David Beckham. His reply was along the lines of 'I feel sorry for the poor lad because his wife can't bloody sing to save her life'.

Mark Wisdom

If it hadn't have been for Brian I would never have been a Derby County fan... although born in the West Midlands as child we moved all around the UK... but in 1969 looking at my Rothmans annual (one for the kids!) I saw Derby at the top of Division Two having won the league by a canter and I thought I'll support them and I have through everything (beating Real Madrid 4-1 at the Baseball Ground to losing to QPR in the play-off final to a last minute goal).

I even spent a few years working at Pride Park (Ipro) Stadium as the stadium sales manager. My son has followed in my footsteps (although he did try and resist) but seeing us get promoted in the play-offs at Wembley a few years ago he's now hooked and drags me along to games.... thank you Brian Clough.. the best ever manager.... I wouldn't... couldn't imagine supporting anybody else apart from the Super Rams

Martin Dempster

Just a few funny memories. He was co-commentating on the UEFA cup final Spurs v Anderlecht when a fan threw a bottle on the pitch. His unique voice calling the bloke an imbecile was cutting but hilarious. The other was him coaching Gazza at White Hart Lane when we played Forest. Putting his arm around him and giving him some advice. Classic Clough!

Dominic Sibley

THE CLUBS BEHIND THE LEGEND

Middlesbrough (1955-61)

Brian began his senior professional career at Boro in 1955. He scored 197 goals in 213 appearances. a striker perhaps not blessed with lightning pace, Clough's fearlessness in front of goal led to two England caps while his team was in the Second Division.

Sunderland (1961-64)

Recruited by Allan Brown in the summer of 1961, Brian continued to score at a rapid rate notching 54 goals in 61 appearances for Sunderland. He started the 1962–63 season by topping the national scoring charts again before a serious knee injury sustained against Bury at Christmas effectively ended his career.

He managed three more games before retiring at 29. He worked as a youth team coach under manager Allan Brown and quickly realised he had a knack for it.

Hartlepool (1965-67)

Brian became Hartlepools United's manager at just 30. It made him the youngest manager in the league at the time. After a fall out with the board he was sacked by chairman Ernie Ord, however a campaign by supporters led to his reinstatement and Ord's resignation. Brian and his assistant Peter Taylor led the team to an 8th place finish. The team gained promotion the year after the pair left for Derby County.

Derby County (1967-73)

Brian and Peter joined Second Division Derby County in 1967. They won the Second Division title in 1969 and later won the Division One title in 1972 in unusual circumstances – with Derby having completed their fixtures the players were on holiday in Spain and Clough was in the Scilly Isles with his family when news came through that Leeds had failed to get the point and Liverpool the win required to deny Derby the title.

The following season Clough took Derby to the semi-finals of the European Cup where many felt a series of questionable refereeing decisions against Juventus saw Derby beaten 3-1 on aggregate.

In October 1973 after questions over Taylor's role, the pair resigned. Clough later admitted it was 'the worst mistake of his life'.

Brighton & Hove Albion (1973-74)

Brian and Peter moved to Brighton after Derby County but the pair won just 12 out of 32 games. Brian left after half a season to become manager of Leeds United while Taylor stayed for a further two seasons narrowly missing promotion in 1975–76.

Leeds United (1974)

Brian joined champions Leeds United after Don Revie accepted the England job. He was sacked after only 44 days having won only one of six league games. His contract pay-off was an estimated £98,000 (about £1m in today's money). His time at Leeds was later controversially fictionalised by writer David Peace in The Damned United, a version of events disputed by the players at Leeds and Brian's family.

Nottingham Forest (1975-93)

Clough moved to Forest in January 1975. His first one and a half seasons at The City Ground were a disappointment but the arrival of Peter Taylor in 1976 changed the club's fortunes around. Promoted in 1977, Forest took the First Division by storm the following season. The signing of Peter Shilton in September proved to be the turning point as Forest won the league title with five games to spare. They also won the League Cup, beating Liverpool 1-0 in a replay.

The following season saw Forest retain the League Cup. In the European Cup they drew Liverpool in the First round and triumphed 2-0 on aggregate. They went on to win the trophy beating Malmo 1-0 in May 1979. They repeated the trick a year later, recovering from a 0-1 deficit to beat Dinamo Berlin in the quarter-finals, Ajax in the semis and Hamburg 1-0 in the final with a John Robertson goal.

Taylor and Clough fell out in 1982 and they very sadly never made up. Taylor went on to manage Derby County and the teams met in the Third Round of the 1983 FA Cup – Derby winning 2-0.

Always renowned for playing good football, Clough's Forest often struggled against the Route One teams of the

First Division in the eighties. There was always a conflict in styles between the likes of Wimbledon and Arsenal and Clough's philosophy of neat football. Yet Brian won two further League Cups in 1989 and 1990 and were often the best of the rest as Liverpool hovered up title after title.

Unfortunately his Forest side lost the 1991 FA Cup final to Tottenham Hotspur. It was the only major trophy that eluded Clough during his managerial career. He left Forest in 1993 after they were relegated.

Year By Year..

1935: Brian born on 21 March in Middlesbrough

1955: Playing debut for Middlesbrough. Scores 204 goals in 222 league matches.

1961: Joins Sunderland for £55,000. Clough scored a total of 63 goals in 74 matches

1962-64: In December 1962, Clough suffered ligament damage in his knee. Two years later he was forced to retire from playing at the age of 29.

1967: Becomes Derby boss after short spell as manager of Hartlepool & wins the 2nd Division title in 1969.

1972: Derby wins First Division title.

1975-77: Joins Nottingham Forest and wins promotion to Division One in 1977.

1978: Wins the First Division title with Nottingham Forest and the League Cup beating Liverpool 1-0 in the replayed final at Old Trafford thanks to a John Robertson penalty.

1979: Wins the European Cup after defeating Malmo 1-0 in the final in Munich, Germany, Trevor Francis with the goal, and Forest also retain the League Cup by beating Southampton 3-2 at Wembley Stadium with goals from Tony Woodcock and a double from Gary Birtles. Wins the European Super Cup by beating Barcelona thanks to a goal by Charlie George in the First Leg at the City Ground winning 1-0, and the return leg in Barcelona finished 1-1, thanks to an equaliser by

Kenny Burns. Forest won 2–1 on Aggregate.

1980: Retains European Cup after beating Hamburg 1-0 in Madrid, Thanks to a John Robertson goal.

1989–1990: Wins back-to-back League Cups in 1989 and 1990, The 1989 final held at Wembley Stadium finished 3-1 against Luton Town, thanks to goals from Neil Webb and a double from Nigel Clough, The 1990 final at Wembley Stadium finished 1-0 thanks to a goal by Nigel Jemson

1993: Leaves Forest after 18 seasons as Forest are relegated after 16 years in the top flight.

2004: Died on 20 September in Derby

The Words Behind The Legend

"Brian Clough's advice to me before most games was: 'you get it, you pass it to another player in a red shirt'. That's really all I've tried to do at Forest and United — pass and move — and I've made a career out of it."

Roy Keane

"That Seaman is a handsome young man but he spends too much time looking in the mirror, rather than at the ball. You can't keep goal with hair like that."

"On occasions I have been big headed. I think most people are when they get in the limelight. I call myself Big Head just to remind myself not to be."

"Walk on water? I know most people out there will be saying that instead of walking on it, I should have taken more of it with my drinks. They are absolutely right."

"I'm sure the England selectors thought if they took me on and gave me the job, I'd want to run the show. They were shrewd, because that's exactly what I would have done."

On Victoria Beckham: "Who the hell wants 14 pairs of shoes when you go on holiday? I haven't had 14 pairs in my life!"

"Players lose you games, not tactics. There's so much crap talked about tactics by people who barely know how to win at dominoes."

"When I go, God's going to have to give up his favourite chair."

"I want no epitaphs of profound history and all that type of thing. I contributed – I would hope they would say that, and I would hope somebody liked me."

"The river Trent is lovely, I know because I have walked on it for 18 years."

"I'm not saying I was the best manager in the business. But I was in the top one."

"I've decided to pick my moment to retire very carefully – in about 200 years time."

"There are more hooligans in the House of Commons than at a football match."

"If God had wanted us to play football in the clouds, he'd have put grass up there."

"Man Utd in Brazil? I hope they all get bloody diarrhea." *On Man Utd being forced to opt-out of the FA Cup to play in the World Club Championship.*

"I can't even spell spaghetti never mind talk Italian. How could I tell an Italian to get the ball – he might grab mine." *On the influx of foreign players.*

"I bet their dressing room will smell of garlic rather than liniment over the next few months." *On the number of French players at Arsenal.*

"Rome wasn't built in a day. But I wasn't on that particular job."

"At last England have appointed a manager who speaks English better than the players." *On the appointment of Sven as England manager.*

"If he'd been English or Swedish, he'd have walked the England job." *On Martin O'Neill.*

"Anybody who can do anything in Leicester but make a jumper has got to be a genius." *A tribute to Martin O'Neill.*

"The ugliest player I ever signed was Kenny Burns."

"Stand up straight, get your shoulders back and get your hair cut." *Advice for John McGovern at Hartlepool.*

"Take your hands out of your pockets." *More advice, this time for a young Trevor Francis as he receives an award from the master Manager.*

"The Derby players have seen more of his balls than the one they're meant to be playing with." *On the streaker who appeared during Derby's game against Manchester United.*

"I only ever hit Roy the once. He got up so I couldn't have hit him very hard." *On dealing with Roy Keane.*

"I'm dealing with my drinking problem and I have a reputation for getting things done."

"Don't send me flowers when I'm dead. If you like me, send them while I'm alive." *After the operation which saved his life.*

"We talk about it for twenty minutes and then we decide I was right." *On dealing with a player who disagrees.*

"It was a crooked match and he was a crooked referee. That was a tournament we could and should have won." *On the 1984 UEFA Cup semi-final Forest loss to Anderlecht.*

"You don't want roast beef and Yorkshire pudding every night and twice on Sunday." *On too much football on television.*

In response to a journalist, "Me telling Roy McFarland to get his haircut, now that is coaching at the top level."

"I'm not saying he's pale and thin but the maid in our hotel room pulled back the sheets and remade the bed without realising he was still in it." *Referring to former Forest player Brian Rice.*

"If a chairman sacks the manager he initially appointed, he should go as well."

"I thought it was my next door neighbour, because I think she felt that if I got something like that, I'd have to move." *Guessing who nominated him for a knighthood.*

"For all his horses, knighthoods and championships, he hasn't got two of what I've got. And I don't mean balls!" *Referring to Sir Alex Ferguson's failure to win successive European Cups.*

"I like my women to be feminine, not sliding into tackles and covered in mud." *On women's football.*

"I've missed him. He used to make me laugh. He was the best diffuser of a situation I have ever known. I hope he's alright." *On the late Peter Taylor.*

"He's learned more about football management than he ever imagined. Some people think you can take football boots off and put a suit on. You can't do that." *On David Platt's first season as Forest manager.*

"He should guide Posh in the direction of a singing coach because she's nowhere near as good at her job as her husband." *Advice for David Beckham*

"Barbara's supervising the move. She's having more extensions built than Heathrow Airport." *On moving house in Derbyshire.*

Childhood

"The most vivid Christmas of all was the year I got the turkey leg. You see, I had a long wait for it, there were 8 in the family and only two legs on the turkey"

"When I was a bairn, in the era of baggy shorts growing up in the North East meant that you were raised on stories of great centre forwards."

"Wilf Mannion was my hero, it was as if he'd walked straight out of the cinema screen. In Middlesbrough he was like a movie star. Hollywood on our streets."

"In the North East the front step of your house was important, it had to be spotless so that you could have eaten your Sunday dinner off it, ours was – it was the best in the street. It gave our Mam a great deal of pride."

"My dad was a football fanatic and he worked in a sweet factory. What else does a boy need!"

"I was taught the importance of clean shoes. Mind you, I had to polish them hard. I wore the toes out of most of them kicking a ball around."

"At school I was a failure, I suppose I was thick... I cried when I failed my 11-Plus."

"At first Middlesbrough thought I was crap – too mouthy, too awkward. The club used that as an excuse not to see what I could do on the pitch"

"Alan Brown influenced me because I respected him so much and he scared me half to death you didn't want to be on the end of one of his bollockings, the first thing he ever said to me was 'you may have heard that I'm a bastard ... well, they're right' and yes he could be, but he was a brilliant one"

"We used to sleep three to a bed. There was me, Our Bill and our Gerald. We were never cold."

"We were beaten 6-3 at Charlton once, I got the three, on the way home I said 'If we score 5 next week, do you think we'll get a point?' That sort of thing didn't go down well with centre halves."

"I always remember trying to get up when the ball broke free. I tried to crawl after it, but I couldn't move ... The Bury centre-half Bob Stokoe was shouting at me: 'Get up ... there's nothing wrong with you'" *On the injury which effectively ended his playing career.*

"I not only did my knee, I banged my head. A lot of people put it down to the way I've behaved for the last ten years."

"He was so wrong because I was a better player than the bloke he took. He was a lad called Derek Kevan and he couldn't play at all compared to my ability" *On Walter Winterbottom's decision to leave him out of the 1958 World Cup squad.*

"I am very happy to have scored 250 league goals faster than anyone else."

"The best thing I ever did in my life. Oh, was I lucky" *On marrying his wife Barbara..*

"Publicity is not my strong suit. Some footballers like to see their name constantly in the headlines. I don't."

"It certainly wasn't luck and I don't mean that conceitedly, cause you can't get lucky 40 times a year. You can get lucky five times, but not 40" *On the fact he regularly scored 40 goals a season.*

Hartlepool

In October 1965, At just 29, Brian became a manager with Peter Taylor as it assistant. He described taking over at Hartlepool as like "Dropping off the end of the world" They nearly always finished near the bottom of the fourth division. The chairman used to ring Brian's office at 4.55pm every day to make sure he hadn't scarpered off early.

"Age doesn't count. It's what you know about football that matters."

"He threatened to sack me at least 43 times a week" *On his first chairman Ernest Ord.*

"It won't be a little place for very long... I know I am better than the 500 or so managers who have been sacked since the war. If they had known anything about the game, they wouldn't have lost their jobs" *On taking over in1965*

"I didn't talk him into coming. I just showed him some pound notes. Two hundred, actually." *On persuading Peter Taylor to join him.*

"I cut the grass and cleaned the drains and even mopped the dressing room floor, we travelled jammed in our own private cars. Fifteen of us went to Barnsley once for £22 – petrol, meals, the lot" *on life At Hartlepool.*

Derby County

"When I first came to Derby, the fans used to say 'He's a cocky bugger' but we started winning things and they put up with me"

"We haven't got a chance of the title!" *They won it a month later.*

"This is one of the miracles of the century, our triumph proves there is hope for all the little people of the world" *After winning the league in 1972*

"No cheating bastards will I talk to, I will not talk to any cheating bastards" *Brian's response to the Italian press after losing in 1973 to Juventus. He thought the referee had been bribed.*

"Taylor began telling the board that the team was so good that even Longson could manage it and Longson began to believe it" *On the reasons for the rift with the board that led to the pair's resignation in 1973.*

"My feelings now are of complete and utter pity for Derby County" *After his resignation in 1973.*

"There have been months of sleepless nights, I know Peter hasn't been sleeping and he knows I haven't been sleeping because we have had to telephone each other to talk about our problems at ridiculous hours" *on the stress of leaving Derby, 1973.*

"I dropped the worst clanger of my career by walking out on Derby, It was an absolute tragedy, I quit without a penny when I should of stayed to fight the blokes on the board who wanted me out."

"If I hadn't of cleared off, if things had been different, Liverpool wouldn't of won all those trophies, Derby would have got there first."

"She came up with one of the wisest and most sensible statements I've ever heard. 'If you go back' she said 'You'd be nuts'" *On not accepting Derby County's offer to return in 1977 after his wife Barbara's advice.*

"I'm sick and tired of being asked whether Derby hold a special place in my heart. They don't."

"Some of my heart, wherever I have wandered, was in Derby… I wish I'd never left. It was the best job I ever had… It's like your first girlfriend. You don't forget, do you?"

Brighton

"All I knew about Brighton was that it had a pier."

"My young lad Nigel would insist on going to school with a Brighton bag. They gave him hell."

"Brighton and I are having an affair and we'll never be right for one another until the day we are married." *On his struggle for points, 1974*

"I didn't make a mistake in going to Brighton, I just went there for the wrong reasons."

Leeds United

"Name your price. You can have whatever you want to come up here and help me, it's too much for one" *To Peter Taylor, who didn't want to join Brian at Leeds, 1974.*

"Chuck your medals in the bin 'cos you won 'em all by cheating." *In his first team meeting at Leeds United, 1974*

"The players have more meetings than the union at Ford." *On dressing room opposition to his methods at Leeds, 1974*

"By next April, whether we win anything or not, I will have proved to Billy Bremner that I'm as good a manager as Don Revie – or better"

"It was 44 days of tension, conflict and unpleasantness … and I wasn't there long enough to find out where to park the car"

"I under-estimated the depth of feeling against me and … I tried to change everything too quickly." *On why he was sacked from Leeds after just 44 days.*

"If the club had stayed loyal, and showed a bit of courage, I'd of given them the one thing Don Revie couldn't get his hands on - The European Cup."

"I remember that I took my cheque straight to the bank, if anyone was that shallow and stupid to sack me after 44 days, I didn't trust them."

"I have been to the extremes in football, I have been to the very top and I've got the sack."

NOTTINGHAM FOREST

"I've left the human race and joined the rat race" *On returning to football after four months away, 1975*

"We couldn't have beaten a team from Come Dancing" *On the Forest team he took over.*

"When I started at Nottingham Forest, there was an empty row of seats at the back of the box - 'cos some idiots were spitting at the committee."

"Gentlemen, No Swearing Please - Brian" *The sign that was erected in front of the Trent End to stop bad language in 1977.*

"I thought we'd do it before Peter arrived, the second he walked through the door, i knew it" *Brian on promotion to the First Division after Peter Taylor rejoined him in the summer of 1976.*

"Not as good as the Derby side and not as close knit" *Comparing Forest to Derby's championship sides.*

"We treat our European matches like seaside holidays, a break from the factory floor of the Football League. We enjoy ourselves, even though we pack our boots rather than a bucket and spade." *On the way to winning the European Cup, 1979.*

"Listen, most of our lot are so young most of 'em still believe in Father Christmas. I haven't the heart to tell them the truth" *On the average age of Forest's team in 1984*

"Our problem isn't injury – it's acne" *Dwelling on the youthfulness of his players.*

"It doesn't affect me. Other people want to win it for me more than I want to win it" *On the FA Cup.*

"Whoever succeeds me at Forest will upset me if he does less than I have done, I want him to win more."

On Nigel Jemson: "I haven't seen the lad but my coaches have and he also comes highly reccommended by my greengrocer"

"No one will ever do what I did at Nottingham Forest. Now that's something to keep you warm at night"

ENGLAND

"I was never going to get that job, But when the FA saw I wasn't the awful, snarling, spitting, bombastic bloke they'd imagined, I took them by utter surprise" *On his interview for the England job in 1977.*

"I'd have tried not to give them the time of day" *On the FA councillors.*

"I might have lasted less than 44 days." *After being asked whether he'd have been a success with England.*

"If the post of England manager had been filled on the basis of outstanding achievement, then Ron Greenwood would not have had a smell."

"If Taylor and I had got that job, we'd of won the bloody thing" *On England in the 1982 World Cup Finals.*

"The chance of England disappeared four years ago. I then resigned myself to never getting the job and withdrawing from all future races." *Reflecting on the one that got away, 1981.*

"I'm fed up with Bobby Robson pointing at his grey hairs and saying that the England Manager's job has aged him 10 years. If he doesn't like it, why doesn't he go back to his orchard in Ipswich?" *1988*

"I just happen to think I'd have been brilliant" *On whether he'd have made a good England manager, 1993*

"They were wrong, you know, I could have done both jobs" *On the Forest board's decision not to allow him to take the Welsh job part-time in 1988.*

"I know there wouldn't be any problems getting across to Dublin. It's just a straight walk across the Irish Sea for me" *On being linked with the Republic Of Ireland manager's job.*

"I want to be manager of Scotland. If I thought for one second the Scottish Football Association would give me the chance, I'd grab it" *1986*

In a TV debate during the 1986 World Cup:

Mick Channon: "We've got to get bodies in the box. The French do it, the Brazilians do it, the Italians do it…"

Clough: "Even educated fleas do it"

PETER TAYLOR

"Without him, my job would be impossible" *1966*

"I object to the word 'Assistant' when he is talked about. He's my partner – the only man in football who can spend big money without the manager's sanction" *1969*

"I'm the shop window, he's the goods at the back" *1971*

"We were arrogant at the bottom and we are arrogant at the top – that's consistency" *1979*

"He wouldn't have shifted a copy without my mug on the front, my name alongside it and my thoughts on every page" *After hearing Peter Taylor had written a book - With Clough, By Taylor - without telling him about it, 1980.*

"He said we've shot it, haven't we?, I said "No, you have!" … But when he sat in his office and told me he wanted to get out of the game, I cried" *When Taylor broke the news of his retirement in 1982*

"One call. Two lines in a letter. That's all it needed" *His lament after Taylor signed John Robertson for Derby without telling him, 1983.*

"'Easy' Barbara said, 'We're going'. Peter Taylor had carried my children on his back" *Asked whether it had been a difficult decision to attend Peter Taylor's funeral, 1992*

OTHER MANAGERS

"Sir Alf has picked the wrong teams, That's all there is to the argument." *On Sir Alf Ramsey's failure to qualify for the World Cup Finals in 1973.*

"Bill Shankly talked more sense about football, than the rest of the Football League put together. Mind you, I'm excluding myself from that assessment" *1974*

"Bill Nicholson used to say that a pat on the back isn't too far from a kick up the arse. He was right!" *On Spurs' double-winning boss, 1982*

"When they gave Kenny (Dalglish) the Anfield manager's job, he didn't just win the pools - he made off with the Crown Jewels" *On the good fortune of being manager of Liverpool, 1987.*

"I hate to mention him because he's a very talented man and I don't like him. I don't like the way he goes about the football either." *On Don Revie, 1974.*

"He was so money-conscious it was incredible. I worked with him in television and do you know what he did when he bought a drink? He wrote it down on a little pad." *On Don Revie, 1984*

"He couldn't keep a clean sheet to save his bloody life" *On Ron Greenwood.*

"I like the look of Mourinho, There's a bit of the young Clough about him." *On Chelsea's Jose Mourinho 2004.*

MANAGEMENT STYLE

"Me? Rely on footballers? That's crap! If I relied on footballers, I would have been out of a job 20 years ago" *1983*

"Players aren't treated like gods here. They are flesh and blood, they never stop learning their craft" *On his philosophy at Nottingham Forest,1979*

"Floats like a butterfly and stings like one too" *On Trevor Brooking,1975*

"When you learn to play with it, you can have the match ball." *To Peter Withe, who had just scored Four goals for Forest v Ipswich, 1977*

"I've bought him to teach the others how to play." *On signing John McGovern for Nottingham Forest 1975*

"Have you ever been hit in the stomach?" *His question to Nigel Jemson - before he hit him in the stomach, 1991*

"I think he's got a lot of talent, and I've asked our coach driver, if he sees him in the tunnel at Wembley, to try and knock him down." *On Paul Gascoigne before the 1991 FA Cup Final.*

"He gets more than me, I only get £200 a week. He gets £250" *On Stuart Pearce, 1989.*

"I'd have cut his balls off!" *On Eric Cantona's Kung Fu Kick, 1995*

"Oh I'd have sent him home alright, but I'd of shot him first." *On Roy Keane leaving the Ireland camp, 2002.*

"Get out of my sight. If I ever see you again, I'll kill you" *To Justin Fashanu, who had just pulled out of a match with an injury 45 minutes before kick off, 1983.*

"Our Elizabeth could have put it in" *On Trevor Francis' winning header in the 1979 European Cup Final,1990.*

"The sins of the father shouldn't be heaped on the shoulders of his son." *On the fear that Nigel would be criticised unfairly because of him, 1986.*

"What is the point of giving you the ball when there is a genius on the other wing?" *Question to Martin O'Neill about John Robertson, 1979.*

"I could point to Robbo and say,: "You were a tramp when I came here, and now you're the best winger in the game." *On John Robertson, 1982*

"When he learns how to trap a ball and kick it, I'll play him" *On Gary Megson 1984*

"He's got bigger dimples than Shirley Temple" *On Teddy Sheringham, 1990*

"He was Derby County … He was better than Bobby Moore" *On Dave Mackay, 1990.*

"He won me the championship, We thought if we scored, we'd win 'cos no one could get the ball past him." *On Peter Shilton,1988*

"The ball is your best friend, Love It, Caress It."

"No one who hasn't done it realises how lonely the job is." *On Management without an assistant,1985*

"I didn't set out to create an image, It was just me, you get what you see with me, and you get what you hear."

"I'm fat, fifty and worn out" *1985*

RETIREMENT

"No wife can have had a more wretched husband, I must have been terrible to live with." *On his marriage, 1968.*

"My wife says it stands for Old Big Ead." *On being awarded the OBE in 1991.*

"After I've been gone for a while, it'll be as if I never existed in football" *1993*

"To put everyone's mind at rest, I'd like to stress that they didn't give me George Best's old liver" *After his own liver transplant, 2003*

"I've had enough and I'm getting out to enjoy what's left of my life."

"I hope when I've gone, people will say I did it right. I played football on the grass."

THE PLAYERS BEHIND THE LEGEND

Brian Clough died in 2004 after a long battle with cancer. Here are a few contemporary reactions to his death.

'There have been some brilliant managers, but for me he was the greatest of all time. What he achieved at two clubs which were totally provincial and not very fashionable, to win two European Cups with Forest after reaching the semi-final with Derby, it was incredible.

'When you look at what happened to us at Forest, winning the old second division one year, the Championship the next and then successive European Cups. I don't know anyone else who could have done that. As far as I'm concerned, he was definitely the best there has ever been. I loved the guy.

'The classic Cloughie story was when Tony Woodcock decided to grow a beard and the gaffer asked what was on his face. Tony said that he just wanted to be a bit different. The gaffer told him if he wanted to be different, he should score a hat-trick on Saturday.'

John Robertson

'I think he is probably the greatest English manager. I don't think he will go down as "one of" the greatest. He is the greatest English manager. I know Sir Alf Ramsey won the World Cup but what he did at Derby and Forest, nobody could hold a candle to that.'

Kenny Burns

'He's probably the greatest manager of all time, not just for

Forest supporters and ex-players, but for football in general. He was just unbelievable in management and in life. He was one of those characters who would walk into a room and there would be an immediate hush. His legacy to football, Nottingham Forest and Derby County will be there forever. He had strange methods that probably wouldn't work today, but they were methods that did work. I think we were the only team who got fined if we didn't go out for a drink on a Friday night'

Garry Birtles

'He was box office — wherever he went. l will be eternally grateful for everything he did for me. He completely broke the mould. He had a totally different style of management from anything I have seen before or since. He looked at the bigger picture and is probably the best manager who ever lived. He was an amazing man.'

Duncan McKenzie

'He was a complete one-off. He was unlike any other manager I had played under. such as Bill Nicholson at Tottenham. His team talks could be quite ferocious but he was unique — a brilliant manager who was respected by everyone who played under him. The way he ran the team was superb and his style was impossible to copy. I doubt there will ever be a manager like him again. It is a sad day for the game and he will be badly missed.'

Dave Mackay

'Brian was a teacher. he taught players how to pass the ball and told them to keep the ball on the floor and to respect authority. He was one of the greatest teachers of the players the game has ever seen. If I ever need memories of Brian I just have to look at my medal cabinet – it's full of them.'

John McGovern

'It was a great honour to work for him, You never knew what would happen. He gave you the confidence to be better than you probably were.'

Neil Webb

'He was one of the big characters in the game. I can't name anyone bigger. It was a different day every day. He brought simplicity and the main thing was respect. I'm eternally grateful for what he did for my career. I earned seventy-six England caps under Brian which says it all really. He made me as a player. When I came back from the 1990 World Cup under a bit of a cloud, he was there with an arm around the shoulder. He knew exactly what to do at the right times.'

Stuart Pearce

'He was a tremendous man-manager — that was his greatest gift. He had a great knack of getting 100 per cent from those who worked with him. He never made it too difficult. He stands with the greatest of all time. He was a football man down to his toes. His achievements will stand comparison with anybody in the game.'

Frank Clark

'Brian was an absolute jewel, a diamond and a genuine, true friend. Many people just thought him outspoken and brash but he was much more than that and the fact that he was never England manager was a travesty. He loved his cricket, understood it and came to see me whenever he had the chance at Middlesbrough, Scarborough and Worksop. It was typical of the man that he didn't go into the committee room but arrived in this tracksuit or shorts and sat in a deckchair among the public. His passing is my loss and I shall miss him dearly.'

Geoffrey Boycott, former England cricket captain

'Clough brought an alchemist's touch to the creation of historic success from fairly modest player resources. Only a moron could attempt to deny that what Clough and his men did from their humble Midlands base was truly glorious. How could bossing Europe be seen as anything less? He was much more than simply a great motivator.'

Hugh McIlvanney, Sunday Times

'Clough's achievements as manager established him firmly in the pantheon of the all-time British greats. But on a wider level, Brian Clough was a genuine original. With his vivid eloquence and willingness to challenge the established order of football, he was the best manager the England team never had, and also a refreshing antidote to many modern managers who deal in platitudes and evasions. Brian Clough never shirked a challenge on or off the field and he made a lot of people laugh along the way.'

Pat Murphy, BBC Sport

'To take one second division club to the championship of the first division can be regarded as talent. To do so with two different clubs looks alarmingly like genius. Clough did this with Derby County and then with Nottingham Forest. His career reached its zenith when he got Forest promoted to the first division, won the first division championship in 1978 and then won the European Cup in both the following years. If you factor in Forest's playing and financial resources, these three years can be regarded as the greatest achievement by any manager of any English club.'

Simon Barnes, The Times

'Clough's greatest gift as a manager was in persuading players dismissed as has-beens and never-weres that they had the potential to take on and beat the best. If Clough had a genius as a manager it was that he never took a player or a job at face value.

'He demanded standards of dress and discipline from his players which would make him unemployable nowadays. He believed that if a player couldn't control a ball and pass it then he shouldn't be a professional in the first place. Ho offered me this gem: "l once told Roy McFarland to get his bloody hair cut. That's coaching at top level."

'He was fond of saying, "I'm a big-head. Not a figurehead" in fact he was both. He was also lovable and impossible, wise and silly, attractive and appalling. He was a pickle of man. Trying to sum him up and coming to terms with his death I am greatly saddened, but I can't help smiling.'

Michael Parkinson

THE GAMES BEHIND THE LEGEND

Five Key Matches In Brian Clough's Managerial Career

11th April 1973 - European Cup Semi-final (1st leg)
JUVENTUS 3 DERBY 1
Altafini 27', 84', Causio 65'; Hector 29'

THIS GAME WAS SAID to have cost Brian Clough the chance of the England job 4 years later. Surrounded by Italian reporters after the final whistle he shouted them down by saying "I will not talk to any cheating bastards" and shut the dressing room door.

Having taken over Derby in 1967 Clough and Taylor moulded a team capable of getting out of the Second Division as runaway champions and then to win the League Championship by a nose ahead of overwhelming favourites Leeds United. Now, standing at the zenith, Clough felt fate turn against him.

From the brief match highlights Juventus score three good goals to Derby's one. It's not a bad score line in an away leg against such illustrious opponents. Yet Derby, whose suspicions had been aroused by seeing Juventus substitute Helmut Haller in deep conversation with the German referee both before the game and at half-time, complained about some of the refereeing decisions, particularly the bookings for McFarland and Gemmill which ruled these two key players out of the second leg. But a look at contemporary reports suggest it could have been even worse as the final minutes of the game saw Causio hit the post and a Morini header cleared off the line. It seems churlish to claim Derby were cheated here.

In the return leg, Derby couldn't find a way past Dino Zoff in the Juventus goal, although Alan Hinton missed a penalty in the 57th minute.

The longer lasting impact was on Clough's psche. Desperate to have another crack at the European Cup following what he perceived to be an injustice, he took on the Leeds job 15 months later for what he later admitted were the wrong reasons.

17th December 1977

MANCHESTER UNITED 0 FOREST 4

Brian Greenhoff 22' (o.g.), Tony Woodcock 25', 88', John Robertson 52'

NEWLY PROMOTED Nottingham Forest went to Old Trafford 2 points ahead of nearest challengers Everton and put on a display that many United watchers still regard as the finest performance by any visitors to the famous old ground.

Playing the counter-attacking brand of football for which they would become famous, Forest sliced United apart. The humiliation started in the 22nd minute when Gemmill's flick was chased down by Tony Woodcock. Although driven wide the Forest striker forced his shot against a post and in off an unlucky Brian Greenhoff. Three minutes later Robertson's low centre somehow fell for Woodcock to net the second. Sustained United pressure couldn't break Forest's defence and in the 52nd minute a United free kick was cleared and fell for

Archie Gemmill. His run and through ball found Robertson who slid the ball past a hapless Paddy Roche. In the closing stages Gemmill found Woodcock who beat Roche with ease.

It was a footballing lesson heeded by United who took apart Everton 6-2 at Goodison in their next game to hand Forest a five point advantage, it was an advantage they would not relinquish as they secured the title with five games to play.

28th May 1980 - European Cup Final (Madrid)

NOTTINGHAM FOREST 1 HAMBURG 0

Robertson 20

FOREST HAD BEEN HANDED the toughest of baptisms in the European Cup in 1978 when they were drawn against Liverpool in the first round. Against the odds and predictions of just about every pundit in the press, Forest came through 2-0 on aggregate and strolled through the rest of the tournament treating European away days as a "break from the shop floor" in Clough's words. The final against Malmo in Munich was an anti-climax, the Swedes were a poor team and Forest had lost O'Neill and Gemmill through injury. Trevor Francis, making his European debut, scored the winner by diving into a shot put arena by the side of the pitch to convert a Robertson cross.

In 1979 Forest were happy-go-lucky away from home again. In the quarter-finals they lost 1-0 at home to Dinamo Berlin but won 3-1 over in Germany. A close run thing in the semis against Ajax set up the final against Kevin Keegan's Hamburg in Madrid.

Underdogs this time, Forest successfully nullified the England captain and set about winning the match – Robertson's slaloming run from the left was capped with a precise finished across the keeper.

The achievement of winning back to back European Cups has since only been performed by the great AC Milan team of the late 80s. For a humble city in the East Midlands to join that elite was an achievement that seems almost impossible to modern eyes.

8th January 1983 - FA Cup Third Round
DERBY COUNTY 2 NOTTINGHAM FOREST 0
Gemmill 67, Hill 84

PETER TAYLOR HAD RETIRED from his Assistant Manager role alongside Clough at Forest in 1982 and surprised many by accepting a new job at Derby a few months later. Yet this meeting was far from the friendly meeting of old pals. Clough felt betrayal by Taylor and the pair would fall out once and for all in May 1983 with the covert move of John Robertson from Nottingham to Derby.

Clough learned of Robertson's departure while on holiday and vowed never to speak to his former pal ever again, a vow he would later come to regret following Taylor's death just 7 years later. At the time his anger spilled out into the press, "If I was driving along the A52 between Derby and Nottingham and saw Taylor broken down, thumbing a lift, I wouldn't pick him up, I'd run him over."

Paired together in the third round of the FA Cup Derby, bottom of Division Two beat second in the First Division Forest comfortably. Former Forest midfielder Archie Gemmill curling in a beautiful free-kick before Andy Hill made sure of victory in the closing stages.

At the final whistle there was no handshake as Clough raced down the tunnel to berate his players in the dressing room. "It had completely blown his mind," defender Willie Young would later say, "I'd never seen him under so much pressure."

Even on the coach Clough was running up and down the coach asking his players "Did you shake hands with that shithouse Taylor?"

It was a sad end to a wonderful friendship.

18th May 1991 - 1991 FA Cup Final (Wembley)

Nottingham Forest 1 Tottenham Hotspur 2 (aet)

Pearce 16; Stewart 55, Walker (o.g.) 94

THE FOREST TEAM of the 80s always seemed strangely out of place. Master craftsmen in a period when hod carriers and nightclub bouncers dominated the English First Division.

Howard Kendall's Everton team of 1984/85 typified the direct game. A forceful, athletic 4-4-2 with Andy Gray and Graeme Sharpe spearheading a midfield that would harry teams to death. By contrast Forest wove pretty patterns on the mud heaps of the First Division, often they were incisive but they lacked steel to go the distance - a proto-type of Wenger's Arsenal if you will.

Yet in the cups Clough's team could still come up trumps. The League Cup remained a favoured stand by, Forest delivering the trophy in 1989 and 1990 against Oldham and Luton Town respectively. Then there was Forest's controversial exit at the hands of Anderlecht in the 1984 UEFA Cup semi-finals, the president of the Belgian club later admitting that he had 'loaned' the referee £200,000 – needless to say Forest saw a 2-0 first leg lead evaporate.

Yet the oldest trophy of the lot had always eluded Clough.

In 1991 he finally seemed to be getting the hang of the FA Cup defeating Crystal Palace, Newcastle, Southampton, Norwich and West Ham on the way to a date with Terry Venables' Spurs at Wembley.

In the most bizarre of starts Paul Gascoigne, hero of Tottenham's semi-final win over rivals Arsenal, lunged feet first into Forest full-back Gary Charles' and was soon stretchered off (not sent off as he should have been) with knee ligament damage from which he would never fully recover. Stuart Pearce scored from the resulting free kick but Spurs soon took a grip of the game, equalising through Paul Stewart before Des Walker put through his own goal in extra-time.

Clough did not venture from his bench after the 90 minutes were up, preferring to allow his coaches to do his bidding while Venables beseeched his players to one final effort.

This wasn't Clough's last Wembley appearance (he lost to Manchester United the following year in the League Cup Final) but it was as close as he got to the FA Cup as a player or manager. He later admitted he should have retired at the final whistle.

THE PARTNER BEHIND THE LEGEND

An Appreciation of Peter Taylor

ONE OF THE MOST important meeting of minds in English football history occured in the unlikely setting of the Ayresome Park dressing room sometime in 1957.

Peter Taylor, then reserve goalkeeper for the Teesiders and was already a shrewd judge of football talent, told reserve centre-forward Brian Clough that he was 'the best centre-forward at the club by miles'. "It was the first time he'd ever spoken to me and I'd never had anyone tell me that," Clough later admitted in his autobiography, "even someone as cocksure of himself as I am needed a colleague to say that".

Soon Clough was in the team and on the way to setting an English record for goals per game. Meanwhile Taylor struggled behind an often leaky defence making 140 appearances in 6 years before departing for Port Vale.

Moving into management Taylor quickly established a reputation by winning the Southern League Cup in 1964 with Burton. A year later Clough recruited Taylor to join him at Hartlepools.

Of Clough Taylor later said "once his playing career was over he was the most miserable I've ever seen him. For the three months he was out of the game he was drinking all day, he didn't seem to know which way to turn".

At Hartlepool, they sorted the wheat from the chaff, in his

own words Clough was "the loud mouth shopkeeper, Taylor the goods in the back". Talent spotting was Taylor's forte but his role didn't convince Hartlepools chairman Ernie Ord so the ex-keeper was listed as 'physio' by Clough. "The sight of his overflowing bucket of water and sponge was comical but the pretense worked... for a while".

Soon the tight-fisted Ord wanted Taylor out but the fans revolted. Never one to back down, it was soon the chairman who was forced out as Clough and Taylor stayed put. However by the following season they had pitched up at Derby County, a club with a history of pretty football but only one trophy, the 1946 FA Cup.

Perhaps Taylor's greatest masterstroke was persuading Clough to get Dave Mackay from Spurs. A lynchpin of the Spurs double-winning side, Mackay was on the verge of returning to Hearts as Assistant Manager when Clough turned up at White Hart Lane asking to speak to him. After much Clough persuasion Mackay was signed up to play as a sweeper in Derby's quest for promotion. It proved a masterful signing.

"The moment we knew it had all changed was when Mackay got the ball from a scramble in our box. While others were yelling 'kick it' or 'get rid' the Scot put his foot on the ball and sent a beautful ball forward, in an instant turning defence into attack." Sitting next to him Taylor purred, "That's why we've bought him".

The pair covered for one another's weaknesses – Taylor was superb at finding or improving the individuals in the team, Clough a superb coach respected by the players as still the best finisher in training. Durban, Hinton, O'Hare, McFarland, Todd, Gemmill – the additions proved relatively inexpensive and telling. Derby, on their tight home ground and grassless pitch, were almost impossible to beat.

Over the next four seasons the pair presided over unprecedented success there. Promotion in 1969 was followed by the League Championship in 1972. The failure to fall short, by a whisker, in Europe led to recriminations about 'cheating Italian bastards' by Clough.

Yet the power the two wielded at Derby soon upset the board. The beginning of the end came following a 1-0 win over Manchester United at Old Trafford. Making a rare appearance in the Directors' Lounge the pair were at the peak of their powers but when Taylor was beckoned by one of the Derby directors and asked to explain his role at the club, Clough took umbrage.

Realising that it was 'us or them' Clough and Taylor decided to submit their resignations in order to shock the board into submission but to their surprise they were accepted by embittered chairman Sam Longson. What followed was one of the most bizarre weeks in footall history as a town revolted against its club.

The players threatened to strike as Clough and Taylor became a focus for protest. During the match against Leicester a week later there was open revolt and unbridled joy when Clough appeared in the main stand to wave farewell. However in the end calm was restored and the pair were out without a penny to their name having resigned.

Taylor's grapevine guided them to Brighton where showbiz impresario Mike Bamber was chairman. Despite the promise of riches and being treated like kings, life on the south coast didn't suit Clough who soon departed for Leeds once Don Revie had taken up the England job. Taylor stayed put, just missing out on promotion with The Seagulls in 1976.

After Clough's 44 day stay at Leeds he had decamped to Nottingham Forest. A lifelong Forest supporter, Taylor quickly jumped at the chance to revive the double act. What followed was one of the most remarkable sequences in football history.

Returning to the player acquisition role, Taylor soon found gems to add to his growing collection, the greatest being the acquistion of Peter Shilton in September 1977. From then on Forest were almost unbeatable for three seasons, winning the league title, two League Cups and two European Cups. It was a remarkable run almost unmatched in English football.

Taylor, who had health problems, retired in the summer of 1982 but returned to manage Derby that November to the shock of many. By now a rift had grown between the pair made worse by Taylor learning that Clough had negotiated a pay rise behind his back during their original spell at Derby.

After Taylor poached John Robertson from Forest in May 1983 the pair never spoke again. In newspaper articles Taylor urged his former friend to retire to spare the chairman of Nottingham Forest the tricky decision but it was clear that the rift would never be healed.

Peter Taylor died on 4th October 1990 in Majorca, Spain. He was 62. Brian Clough attended the funeral and bitterly regretted the pair's split for the rest of his life.

APPENDIX

Brian Howard Clough

Born: 21st March 1935, Middlesbrough

Died: 20th September 2004, Derby

Married: Barbara Glasgow – 4th April 1959 (died 2013).

Father of Simon (b.1964), Nigel (b. 1966) and Elizabeth (b. 1967).

More In Detail ...

Brian Clough was in management from 1965 to 1993, Cloughie's career as a player was very prolific, he scored 251 goals in 274 apps, what a great record!

Cloughie also won two England caps, both in 1959, pity he had to retire at 29 years of age after sustaining anterior cruciate ligament damage.

Cloughie ended his career with the highest goals to games ratio of any striker in English football who has scored 200 goals or more.

In 1965, Brian Clough took the manager's job at Fourth Division Hartlepools United, In 1967 Cloughie moved on to Second Division Derby County, In 1968–69 they were Second Division champions

Three years later, Derby County were crowned champions of England for the very first time.

In 1973 the Rams reached the semi-finals of the European Cup but Clough's relationship with the chairman Mr Longson deteriorated and he resigned.

After Derby County, Cloughie spent 8 months at Brighton before spending 44 days at Leeds United in 1974.

Within months Brian had joined second division Nottingham Forest, re-uniting with Peter Taylor in 1976

In 1977, Nottingham Forest were promoted to the top flight and the following season won the league title (the club's first) and that triumph made Brian one of only four managers to win the English League with two different clubs.

Nottingham Forest also won consecutive European Cups (in 1979 & 1980) and League Cups (1978 & 1979) before Peter Taylor retired in 1982.

Brian Clough stayed on as Nottingham Forest manager for another decade and won two more League Cups (1989 & 1990) but could not emulate his earlier successes. Nottingham Forest were relegated from the Premier League in 1993, after which Brian Clough retired from football.

Cloughie's teams were always known for playing attractive football and known for good sportsmanship on the field. Despite Brian being interview for the England National Manager's position in 1977 he was never offered it.

It's always been said (usually by the man himself!) that Cloughie is the greatest manager England never had.

Going back to Cloughie's childhood he once said " I adored it in all its aspects. If anyone should be grateful for their upbringing, for their mam and dad, I'm that person. I was the kid who came from a little part of paradise." Clough claimed that Middlesbrough was not the nicest place in the world but to him it was heaven.

In his school life, he admitted in his autobiography that he had neglected his lessons in favour of sport, surprisingly his first love as a youngster was cricket rather than football.

When he left school he began to work at ICI before doing his National Service in the RAF between 1953-55.

HONOURS

PLAYER

Middlesbrough FC: 1955-1961

Debut: v Barnsley – September 17th 1955.
Scored 197 goals in 213 league games
First league goal: Middlesbrough v Leicester City at Ayresome Park, October 8th, 1955.

Sunderland FC: 1961-1964.

Joined club in July 1961 for £45,000.
Debut v Walsall in August 1961.
54 goals in 61 league games.
Injured v Bury at Roker Park, Boxing Day, 1962.
Became the fastest player to 250 goals.
Retired through injury in November 1964 and joined the club's coaching staff.
Last league goal: Sunderland v Leeds United at Roker Park, September 5th, 1964.

INTERNATIONAL

England caps:
1959 v Wales (Ninian Park); v Sweden (Wembley)

MANAGEMENT

Hartlepools United: October 1965 - May 1967.

Derby County: June 1967 - October 1973.

1968-69: Div 2 Champions;

1971-72: League Champions;

1972-73: European Cup semi-finalists

Brighton And Hove Albion: November 1973 - July 1974

Leeds Utd: August - September 1974.

Nottingham Forest: January 1975 - May 1993

1976-77: Div 2 promotion;

1977-78: League Champions, League Cup winners;

1978-79: European Cup, League Cup, League runners-up

1979-80: European Cup, European Super Cup, World Club finalists, League Cup finalists

1980-81: European Super Cup finalists, World Club finalists

1988-89: League Cup winners, Simod Cup winners

1989-90: League Cup winners

1990-91: FA Cup finalists

1991-92 Zenith Data Cup winners, League Cup finalists

THE NUMBERS BEHIND THE LEGEND

Playing Career

SEASON	CLUB	LEVEL	LEAGUE		FA CUP		LEAGUE CUP	
			APPS	GLS	APPS	GLS	APPS	GLS
1955-56	Middlesbrough	Division Two	9	3				
1956-57	Middlesbrough	Division Two	41	38	3	2		
1957-58	Middlesbrough	Division Two	40	40	2	2		
1958-59	Middlesbrough	Division Two	42	43	1	1		
1959-60	Middlesbrough	Division Two	41	39	1	1		
1960-61	Middlesbrough	Division Two	40	34	1	1	1	1
1961-62	Sunderland	Division Two	34	29	4	0	5	5
1962-63	Sunderland	Division Two	24	24	-	-	4	5
1964-65	Sunderland	Division One	3	1	-	-	-	-
TOTAL			274	251	12	7	10	11

HONOURS	CAPS	GLS
England U23	3	1
England B	1	1
England	2	0

Management Career

CLUB	PERIOD IN CHARGE	P	W	D	L	%
HARTLEPOOLS UNITED	1/10/1965 to 1/5/1967	84	35	13	36	41.67
DERBY COUNTY	1/6/1967 to 15/10/1973	289	135	70	84	46.71
BRIGHTON & HOVE ALBION	1/11/1973 to 30/7/1974	32	12	8	12	37.50
LEEDS UNITED	30/7/1974 to 12/9/1974	7	1	3	3	14.29
NOTTINGHAM FOREST	6 /1/1975 to 8/51993	907	411	246	250	45.31
	Total	1319	594	340	385	45.03

THE TOP ONE?

To build two modest clubs into champions and, in Forest's case European champions, seems sufficient to ensure Clough is at or very near the top of the tree. Indeed he may be the greatest ever – Clough never had the advantage of being able to spend his way out of trouble and it is tempting to speculate how he would have got on at a big club. Anyway, here are the records of some of the greatest managers in English football and how they compare to Brian's record (opposite).

SIR ALEX FERGUSON

HONOURS

MANCHESTER UNITED (28) - 2 World Club Cup, 1 Super Cup, 2 European Cup, 1 Cup Winners Cup, 13 Premier League, 5 FA Cup, 4 League Cup.

MANCHESTER UNITED 1986 -2013

G	W	D	L	WIN %
1,500	895	338	267	59.67

BOB PAISLEY

HONOURS:

LIVERPOOL (14) - 3 European Cup, 1 UEFA Cup, 1 Super Cup, 6 First Division, 3 League Cup.

LIVERPOOL 1974-1983

G	W	D	L	WIN %
535	308	131	96	57.57

BILL SHANKLY

HONOURS - LIVERPOOL (6) - 1 UEFA Cup, 3 First Division titles, 2 FA Cup

LIVERPOOL 1959-1974

G	W	D	L	WIN %
753	393	185	175	52.19

SIR MATT BUSBY

HONOURS: MANCHESTER UNITED (8) 1 European Cup, 5 First Division titles, 2 FA Cup

MANCHESTER UNITED 1945-1971

G	W	D	L	WIN%
1,132	576	266	299	50.45

Hartlepools United

1965-66

Sat 02 Oct 1965	Chesterfield	H	League	L 1-2
Mon 04 Oct 1965	Barrow	A	League	L 0-2
Sat 09 Oct 1965	Tranmere Rovers	H	League	D 0-0
Sat 16 Oct 1965	Colchester United	A	League	L 0-2
Sat 23 Oct 1965	Barnsley	H	League	L 1-2
Sat 30 Oct 1965	Bradford City	A	League	W 3-1
Sat 06 Nov 1965	Crewe Alexandra	H	League	W 4-1
Sat 13 Nov 1965	Workington	H	FAC 1	W 3-1
Sat 20 Nov 1965	Halifax Town	H	League	L 1-2
Sat 27 Nov 1965	Chester	A	League	L 0-2
Sat 04 Dec 1965	Wrexham	h	FAC 2	W 2-0
Sat 11 Dec 1965	Lincoln City	A	League	L 1-2
Sat 18 Dec 1965	Colchester United	H	League	L 0-1
Mon 27 Dec 1965	Darlington	H	League	D 1-1
Tue 28 Dec 1965	Darlington	A	League	D 1-1
Sat 01 Jan 1966	Tranmere Rovers	A	League	L 1-6
Sat 08 Jan 1966	Port Vale	H	League	W 2-0
Sat 15 Jan 1966	Barnsley	A	League	D 2-2
Tues 24 Jan 1966	Huddersfield	A	FAC 3	L 1-3
Sat 29 Jan 1966	Southport	A	League	L 1-4
Sat 05 Feb 1966	Wrexham	H	League	W 4-2
Sat 12 Feb 1966	Luton Town	A	League	L 1-2
Sat 26 Feb 1966	Aldershot	H	League	W 3-0
Sat 05 Mar 1966	Luton Town	H	League	W 2-0
Sat 12 Mar 1966	Newport County	A	League	L 0-3
Sat 19 Mar 1966	Torquay United	H	League	L 0-2
Mon 21 Mar 1966	Port Vale	A	League	D 0-0
Fri 25 Mar 1966	Chesterfield	A	League	W 3-1
Fri 01 Apr 1966	Crewe Alexandra	A	League	L 1-3
Fri 08 Apr 1966	Stockport County	H	League	W 2-1
Sat 09 Apr 1966	Notts. County	H	League	W 2-0
Mon 11 Apr 1966	Stockport County	A	League	W 2-1
Fri 15 Apr 1966	Halifax Town	A	League	L 0-1
Tue 19 Apr 1966	Bradford P A	A	League	L 1-4
Sat 23 Apr 1966	Chester	H	League	W 2-0
Tue 26 Apr 1966	Rochdale	A	League	L 1-3
Sat 30 Apr 1966	Notts. County	A	League	L 0-1
Sat 07 May 1966	Lincoln City	H	League	W 3-1
Mon 09 May 1966	Barrow	H	League	W 3-0
Mon 16 May 1966	Rochdale	H	League	D 0-0
Sat 21 May 1966	Bradford City	H	League	D 1-1

DIVISION FOUR

1	Doncaster Rovers	46	24	11	11	85	54	59
2	Darlington	46	25	9	12	72	53	59
3	Torquay United	46	24	10	12	72	49	58
4	Colchester United	46	23	10	13	70	47	56
5	Tranmere Rovers	46	24	8	14	93	66	56
6	Luton Town	46	24	8	14	90	70	56
7	Chester	46	20	12	14	79	70	52
8	Notts County	46	19	12	15	61	53	50
9	Newport County	46	18	12	16	75	75	48
10	Southport	46	18	12	16	68	69	48
11	Bradford Park Avenue	46	21	5	20	102	92	47
12	Barrow	46	16	15	15	72	76	47
13	Stockport County	46	18	6	22	71	70	42
14	Crewe Alexandra	46	16	9	21	61	63	41
15	Halifax Town	46	15	11	20	67	75	41
16	Barnsley	46	15	10	21	74	78	40
17	Aldershot	46	15	10	21	75	84	40
18	Hartlepools United	46	16	8	22	63	75	40
19	Port Vale	46	15	9	22	48	59	39
20	Chesterfield	46	13	13	20	62	78	39
21	Rochdale	46	16	5	25	71	87	37
22	Lincoln City	46	13	11	22	57	82	37
23	Bradford City	46	12	13	21	63	94	37
24	Wrexham	46	13	9	24	72	104	35

SQUAD: Barry Ashworth, John Bates, Willie Bradley, Bobby Brass, Jimmy Cooper, Brian Drysdale, Ambrose Fogarty, Alan Fox, John Gill, Brian Grant, Les Green, Hugh Hamilton, Eric Harrison, Joe Livingstone , Billy Marshall, John McGovern, Bobby McLeod, Willie Mcpheat, Jim Mulvaney, Tony Parry, Earnie Phythian, Ken Simpkins, John Small, Stan Storton, Peter Thompson, Cliff Wright.

1966-67

Sat 20 Aug 1966	Aldershot	A	League	D 1-1
Wed 23 Aug 1966	Bradford Park Avenue	H	LC 1	D 2-2
Sat 27 Aug 1966	Wrexham	H	League	W 2-1
Wed 31 Aug 1966	Bradford Park Avenue	A	LC1 R	L 1-2
Fri 02 Sep 1966	Southend United	A	League	L 0-2
Mon 05 Sep 1966	Barrow	H	League	W 2-1
Sat 10 Sep 1966	Tranmere Rovers	H	League	L 0-2
Sat 17 Sep 1966	Bradford City	A	League	L 0-3
Mon 19 Sep 1966	Newport County	H	League	L 0-1
Sat 24 Sep 1966	Exeter City	H	League	W 3-1
Mon 26 Sep 1966	Barrow	A	League	W 3-2
Sat 01 Oct 1966	Crewe Alexandra	H	League	L 1-2
Fri 07 Oct 1966	York City	A	League	D 1-1
Sat 15 Oct 1966	Lincoln City	H	League	W 5-0
Mon 17 Oct 1966	Newport County	A	League	W 2-0
Sat 22 Oct 1966	Chesterfield	A	League	L 0-1
Sat 29 Oct 1966	Stockport County	H	League	W 1-0
Sat 05 Nov 1966	Rochdale	A	League	L 2-3
Sat 12 Nov 1966	Southport	H	League	D 1-1
Sat 19 Nov 1966	Notts. County	A	League	D 0-0
Sat 26 Nov 1966	Shrewsbury	A	FAC 1	L 2-5
Sat 03 Dec 1966	Bradford Park Avenue	A	League	W 2-1
Sat 10 Dec 1966	Port Vale	H	League	W 2-1
Sat 17 Dec 1966	Aldershot	H	League	W 3-2
Mon 26 Dec 1966	Brentford	H	League	D 2-2
Tue 27 Dec 1966	Brentford	A	League	W 2-1
Sat 31 Dec 1966	Wrexham	A	League	L 1-4
Fri 06 Jan 1967	Southend United	H	League	L 1-2
Fri 13 Jan 1967	Tranmere Rovers	A	League	L 0-2
Sat 21 Jan 1967	Bradford City	H	League	W 1-0
Mon 30 Jan 1967	Chester	H	League	W 3-2
Sat 04 Feb 1967	Exeter City	A	League	L 0-1
Sat 11 Feb 1967	Crewe Alexandra	A	League	W 2-1
Sat 18 Feb 1967	Barnsley	H	League	D 1-1
Sat 25 Feb 1967	York City	H	League	W 4-2
Sat 04 Mar 1967	Lincoln City	A	League	L 0-3
Sat 11 Mar 1967	Barnsley	A	League	W 2-1
Sat 18 Mar 1967	Chesterfield	H	League	W 3-2
Fri 24 Mar 1967	Luton Town	H	League	W 2-1
Sat 25 Mar 1967	Chester	A	League	L 0-1
Mon 27 Mar 1967	Luton Town	A	League	W 2-0

Sat 01 Apr 1967	Rochdale	H	League	W 2-1
Sat 08 Apr 1967	Southport	A	League	L 1-3
Tue 11 Apr 1967	Halifax Town	A	League	L 1-2
Sat 15 Apr 1967	Notts. County	H	League	W 2-1
Fri 21 Apr 1967	Stockport County	A	League	L 0-2
Mon 24 Apr 1967	Halifax Town	H	League	L 1-3
Sat 29 Apr 1967	Bradford Park Avenue	H	League	W 2-0
Sat 06 May 1967	Port Vale	A	League	D 0-0

DIVISION FOUR

1	Stockport County	46	26	12	8	69	42	64
2	Southport	46	23	13	10	69	42	59
3	Barrow	46	24	11	11	76	54	59
4	Tranmere Rovers	46	22	14	10	66	43	58
5	Crewe Alexandra	46	21	12	13	70	55	54
6	Southend United	46	22	9	15	70	49	53
7	Wrexham	46	16	20	10	76	62	52
8	Hartlepools United	46	22	7	17	66	64	51
9	Brentford	46	18	13	15	58	56	49
10	Aldershot	46	18	12	16	72	57	48
11	Bradford City	46	19	10	17	74	62	48
12	Halifax Town	46	15	14	17	59	68	44
13	Port Vale	46	14	15	17	55	58	43
14	Exeter City	46	14	15	17	50	60	43
15	Chesterfield	46	17	8	21	60	63	42
16	Barnsley	46	13	15	18	60	64	41
17	Luton Town	46	16	9	21	59	73	41
18	Newport County	46	12	16	18	56	63	40
19	Chester	46	15	10	21	54	78	40
20	Notts County	46	13	11	22	53	72	37
21	Rochdale	46	13	11	22	53	75	37
22	York City	46	12	11	23	65	79	35
23	Bradford Park Avenue	46	11	13	22	52	79	35
24	Lincoln City	46	9	13	24	58	82	31

SQUAD: Stan Aston, Terry Bell, John Beresford, Tony Birchamshaw, Albert Broadbent, Brian Drysdale, Ambrose Fogarty, John Gill, Brian Grant, Les Green, John Joyce, Joe Livingstone , John McGovern, Bobby McLeod, Jim Mulvaney, Tony Parry, Earnie Phythian, John Sheridan, Ken Simpkins, Mick Somers, Cliff Wright.

DERBY COUNTY

1967-68

Sat 19 Aug 1967	Charlton Athletic	H	League	W 3-2
Sat 26 Aug 1967	Crystal Palace	A	League	L 0-1
Mon 28 Aug 1967	Rotherham United	A	League	W 3-1
Sat 02 Sep 1967	Aston Villa	H	League	W 3-1
Wed 06 Sep 1967	Norwich City	A	League	L 2-3
Sat 09 Sep 1967	Queens Park Rangers	A	League	W 1-0
Wed 13 Sep 1967	Hartlepools United	H	LC 2	W 4-0
Sat 16 Sep 1967	Plymouth Argyle	H	League	W 1-0
Sat 23 Sep 1967	Cardiff City	A	League	W 5-1
Wed 27 Sep 1967	Rotherham United	H	League	W 4-1
Sat 30 Sep 1967	Portsmouth	H	League	L 0-1
Sat 07 Oct 1967	Millwall	H	League	D 3-3
Wed 11 Oct 1967	Birmingham City	H	LC 3	W 3-1
Sat 14 Oct 1967	Ipswich Town	A	League	L 0-4
Sat 21 Oct 1967	Huddersfield Town	H	League	W 1-0
Sat 28 Oct 1967	Bolton Wanderers	A	League	L 3-5
Wed 01 Nov 1967	Lincoln City	H	LC 4	D 0-0
Sat 04 Nov 1967	Birmingham City	H	League	D 2-2
Fri 10 Nov 1967	Bristol City	A	League	L 0-1
Wed 15 Nov 1967	Lincoln City	A	LC 4 Replay	W 3-0
Sat 18 Nov 1967	Carlisle United	H	League	L 0-1
Sat 25 Nov 1967	Hull City	A	League	L 0-3
Wed 29 Nov 1967	Darlington	H	LC 5	W 5-4
Sat 02 Dec 1967	Middlesbrough	H	League	L 2-4
Sat 09 Dec 1967	Blackpool	A	League	D 1-1
Sat 16 Dec 1967	Charlton Athletic	A	League	W 2-1
Sat 23 Dec 1967	Crystal Palace	H	League	D 1-1
Tue 26 Dec 1967	Blackburn Rovers	A	League	L 0-3
Sat 30 Dec 1967	Blackburn Rovers	H	League	D 2-2
Sat 06 Jan 1968	Aston Villa	A	League	L 1-2
Wed 17 Jan 1968	Leeds United	H	LC SF 1L	L 0-1
Sat 20 Jan 1968	Plymouth Argyle	A	League	W 4-3
Sat 27 Jan 1968	Leeds United	A	FAC 3	L 0-2
Sat 03 Feb 1968	Cardiff City	H	League	L 3-4
Wed 07 Feb 1968	Leeds United	A	LC SF 2L	L 2-3
Sat 10 Feb 1968	Portsmouth	A	League	L 2-3
Sat 17 Feb 1968	Queens Park Rangers	H	League	W 4-0
Sat 24 Feb 1968	Millwall	A	League	D 1-1
Sat 02 Mar 1968	Ipswich Town	H	League	L 2-3
Sat 09 Mar 1968	Norwich City	H	League	D 1-1
Sat 16 Mar 1968	Huddersfield Town	A	League	L 1-3
Sat 23 Mar 1968	Bolton Wanderers	H	League	W 2-1

Tue 02 Apr 1968	Birmingham City	A	League	L 1-3
Sat 06 Apr 1968	Bristol City	H	League	W 3-1
Sat 13 Apr 1968	Carlisle United	A	League	D 1-1
Mon 15 Apr 1968	Preston North End	H	League	L 1-2
Tue 16 Apr 1968	Preston North End	A	League	D 1-1
Sat 20 Apr 1968	Hull City	H	League	L 1-2
Sat 27 Apr 1968	Middlesbrough	A	League	D 2-2
Sat 04 May 1968	Blackpool	H	League	L 1-3

DIVISION TWO

1	Ipswich Town	42	22	15	5	79	44	59
2	Queens Park Rangers	42	25	8	9	67	36	58
3	Blackpool	42	24	10	8	71	43	58
4	Birmingham City	42	19	14	9	81	51	52
5	Portsmouth	42	18	13	11	68	55	49
6	Middlesbrough	42	17	12	13	60	54	46
7	Millwall	42	14	17	11	62	50	45
8	Blackburn Rovers	42	16	11	15	56	49	43
9	Norwich City	42	16	11	15	60	65	43
10	Carlisle United	42	14	13	15	58	52	41
11	Crystal Palace	42	14	11	17	56	56	39
12	Bolton Wanderers	42	13	13	16	60	63	39
13	Cardiff City	42	13	12	17	60	66	38
14	Huddersfield Town	42	13	12	17	46	61	38
15	Charlton Athletic	42	12	13	17	63	68	37
16	Aston Villa	42	15	7	20	54	64	37
17	Hull City	42	12	13	17	58	73	37
18	Derby County	42	14	7	21	50	73	36
19	Bristol City	42	13	10	19	48	62	36
20	Preston North End	42	12	11	19	43	65	35
21	Rotherham United	42	10	11	21	42	76	31
22	Plymouth Argyle	42	9	9	24	38	72	27

SQUAD: Richie Barker , Colin Boulton, Barry Butlin, Ian Buxton, Peter Daniel, Alan Durban, Kevin Hector, Alan Hinton, Billy Hodgson, Mick Hopkinson, Gordon Hughes, Reg Matthews, Roy McFarland, John O'Hare, Tony Rhodes, John Richardson, John Robson, Bobby Saxton, Arthur Stewart, Eddie Thomas, Jim Walker, Phil Waller, Ron Webster, Pat Wright,

1968-69

Sat 10 Aug 1968	Blackburn Rovers	A	League	D 1-1
Tues 13 Aug 1968	Chesterfield	H	LC 1	W 3-0
Sat 17 Aug 1968	Blackpool	H	League	D 1-1
Tue 20 Aug 1968	Sheffield United	A	League	L 0-2
Sat 24 Aug 1968	Huddersfield Town	A	League	L 0-2
Wed 28 Aug 1968	Hull City	H	League	D 2-2
Sat 31 Aug 1968	Oxford United	H	League	W 2-0
Wed 04 Sep 1968	Stockport Count	H	LC 2	W 5-1
Sat 07 Sep 1968	Aston Villa	H	League	W 3-1
Sat 14 Sep 1968	Bristol City	A	League	D 0-0
Wed 18 Sep 1968	Fulham	H	League	W 1-0
Sat 21 Sep 1968	Millwall	H	League	W 1-0
Wed 25 Sep 1968	Chelsea	A	LC 3	D 0-0
Sat 28 Sep 1968	Bolton Wanderers	A	League	W 2-1
Wed 02 Oct 1968	Chelsea	H	LC 3 R	W 3-1
Sat 05 Oct 1968	Middlesbrough	A	League	D 0-0
Wed 09 Oct 1968	Hull City	A	League	L 0-1
Sat 12 Oct 1968	Preston North End	H	League	W 1-0
Wed 16 Oct 1968	Everton	A	LC 4	D 0-0
Sat 19 Oct 1968	Portsmouth	A	League	W 1-0
Wed 23 oct 1968	Everton	H	LC 4 R	W 1-0
Sat 26 Oct 1968	Birmingham City	H	League	W 1-0
Wed 30 Oct 1968	Swindon Town	H	LC 5	D 0-0
Wed 05 Nov 1968	Swindon Town	A	LC 5 R	L 0-1
Sat 09 Nov 1968	Charlton Athletic	H	League	W 2-1
Sat 16 Nov 1968	Cardiff City	A	League	D 1-1
Sat 23 Nov 1968	Carlisle United	H	League	D 3-3
Sat 30 Nov 1968	Crystal Palace	A	League	W 2-1
Sat 07 Dec 1968	Norwich City	H	League	D 1-1
Sat 14 Dec 1968	Preston North End	A	League	D 0-0
Sat 21 Dec 1968	Portsmouth	H	League	W 2-1
Thu 26 Dec 1968	Middlesbrough	H	League	W 3-2
Sat 04 Jan 1969	Burnley	A	FAC 3	L 1-3
Sat 11 Jan 1969	Bury	H	League	W 2-0
Tue 14 Jan 1969	Birmingham City	A	League	D 1-1
Sat 18 Jan 1969	Charlton Athletic	A	League	L 0-2
Sat 25 Jan 1969	Bury	A	League	W 1-0
Sat 01 Feb 1969	Cardiff City	H	League	W 2-0
Sat 01 Mar 1969	Blackburn Rovers	H	League	W 4-2
Wed 05 Mar 1969	Crystal Palace	H	League	L 0-1

Sat 08 Mar 1969	Blackpool	A	League	W 3-2
Tue 11 Mar 1969	Carlisle United	A	League	D 1-1
Sat 15 Mar 1969	Huddersfield Town	H	League	W 1-0
Sat 22 Mar 1969	Oxford United	A	League	W 2-0
Sat 29 Mar 1969	Aston Villa	A	League	W 1-0
Wed 02 Apr 1969	Fulham	A	League	W 1-0
Sat 05 Apr 1969	Bolton Wanderers	H	League	W 5-1
Mon 07 Apr 1969	Sheffield United	H	League	W 1-0
Sat 12 Apr 1969	Millwall	A	League	W 1-0
Wed 16 Apr 1969	Norwich City	A	League	W 4-1
Sat 19 Apr 1969	Bristol City	H	League	W 5-0

DIVISION TWO

1	Derby County	42	26	11	5	65	32	63
2	Crystal Palace	42	22	12	8	70	47	56
3	Charlton Athletic	42	18	14	10	61	52	50
4	Middlesbrough	42	19	11	12	58	49	49
5	Cardiff City	42	20	7	15	67	54	47
6	Huddersfield Town	42	17	12	13	53	46	46
7	Birmingham City	42	18	8	16	73	59	44
8	Blackpool	42	14	15	13	51	41	43
9	Sheffield United	42	16	11	15	61	50	43
10	Millwall	42	17	9	16	57	49	43
11	Hull City	42	13	16	13	59	52	42
12	Carlisle United	42	16	10	16	46	49	42
13	Norwich City	42	15	10	17	53	56	40
14	Preston North End	42	12	15	15	38	44	39
15	Portsmouth	42	12	14	16	58	58	38
16	Bristol City	42	11	16	15	46	53	38
17	Bolton Wanderers	42	11	16	15	55	67	38
18	Aston Villa	42	12	14	16	37	48	38
19	Blackburn Rovers	42	13	11	18	52	63	37
20	Oxford United	42	12	9	21	34	55	33
21	Bury	42	11	8	23	51	80	30
22	Fulham	42	7	11	24	40	81	25

SQUAD: Richie Barker , Colin Boulton, Barry Butlin, Willie Carlin, Peter Daniel, Alan Durban, Les Green, Kevin Hector, Alan Hinton, Dave Mackay, Roy McFarland, John McGovern, John O'Hare, Tony Rhodes, John Richardson, John Robson, Arthur Stewart, Jim Walker, Ron Webster, Frank Wignall.

1969-70

Sat 09 Aug 1969	Burnley	H	League	D 0-0
Tue 12 Aug 1969	Ipswich Town	A	League	W 1-0
Sat 16 Aug 1969	Coventry City	A	League	D 1-1
Wed 20 Aug 1969	Ipswich Town	H	League	W 3-1
Sat 23 Aug 1969	Stoke City	H	League	D 0-0
Wed 27 Aug 1969	Wolverhampton Wanderers	A	League	D 1-1
Sat 30 Aug 1969	West Bromwich Albion	A	League	W 2-0
Sat 03 Sep 1969	Hartlepool Utd	A	LC 2	W 3-1
Sat 06 Sep 1969	Everton	H	League	W 2-1
Wed 10 Sep 1969	Southampton	H	League	W 3-0
Sat 13 Sep 1969	Newcastle United	A	League	W 1-0
Sat 20 Sep 1969	Tottenham Hotspur	H	League	W 5-0
Wed 24 Sep 1969	Hull City	H	LC 3	W 3-1
Sat 27 Sep 1969	Sheffield Wednesday	A	League	L 0-1
Sat 04 Oct 1969	Manchester United	H	League	W 2-0
Wed 08 Oct 1969	Coventry City	H	League	L 1-3
Sat 11 Oct 1969	Chelsea	A	League	D 2-2
Wed 14 Oct 1969	Crystal Palace	A	LC 4	D 1-1
Sat 18 Oct 1969	Manchester City	H	League	L 0-1
Sat 25 Oct 1969	Leeds United	A	League	L 0-2
Wed 29 Oct 1969	Crystal Palace	H	LC 4 R	W 3-0
Sat 01 Nov 1969	Liverpool	H	League	W 4-0
Sat 08 Nov 1969	Arsenal	A	League	L 0-4
Wed 12 Nov 1969	Manchester United	H	LC 5	D 0-0
Sat 15 Nov 1969	Sunderland	H	League	W 3-0
Wed 19 Nov 1969	Manchester United	A	LC 5 R	L 0-1
Sat 22 Nov 1969	West Ham United	A	League	L 0-3
Sat 29 Nov 1969	Nottingham Forest	H	League	L 0-2
Sat 06 Dec 1969	Crystal Palace	A	League	W 1-0
Sat 13 Dec 1969	Newcastle United	H	League	W 2-0
Sat 20 Dec 1969	Everton	A	League	L 0-1
Fri 26 Dec 1969	Stoke City	A	League	L 0-1
Sat 27 Dec 1969	West Bromwich Albion	H	League	W 2-0
Sat 03 Jan 1970	Preston Ne	A	FAC 3	D 1-1
Wed 07 Jan 1970	Preston Ne	H	FAC 3 R	W 4-1
Sat 10 Jan 1970	Tottenham Hotspur	A	League	L 1-2
Sat 17 Jan 1970	Sheffield Wednesday	H	League	W 1-0
Sat 24 jan 1970	Sheffield United	H	FAC 4	W 3-0
Sat 31 Jan 1970	Manchester United	A	League	L 0-1
Sat 07 Feb 1970	QPR	A	FAC 5	L 0-1
Wed 11 Feb 1970	Chelsea	H	League	D 2-2
Sat 14 Feb 1970	Burnley	A	League	D 1-1
Sat 21 Feb 1970	Arsenal	H	League	W 3-2
Sat 28 Feb 1970	Liverpool	A	League	W 2-0

Sat 07 Mar 1970	West Ham United	H	League	W 3-0
Sat 14 Mar 1970	Nottingham Forest	A	League	W 3-1
Sat 21 Mar 1970	Crystal Palace	H	League	W 3-1
Fri 27 Mar 1970	Manchester City	A	League	W 1-0
Sat 28 Mar 1970	Sunderland	A	League	D 1-1
Mon 30 Mar 1970	Leeds United	H	League	W 4-1
Sat 04 Apr 1970	Wolverhampton Wanderers	H	League	W 2-0
Wed 15 Apr 1970	Southampton	A	League	D 1-1

DIVISION ONE

1	Everton	42	29	8	5	72	34	66
2	Leeds United	42	21	15	6	84	49	57
3	Chelsea	42	21	13	8	70	50	55
4	Derby County	42	22	9	11	64	37	53
5	Liverpool	42	20	11	11	65	42	51
6	Coventry City	42	19	11	12	58	48	49
7	Newcastle United	42	17	13	12	57	35	47
8	Manchester United	42	14	17	11	66	61	45
9	Stoke City	42	15	15	12	56	52	45
10	Manchester City	42	16	11	15	55	48	43
11	Tottenham Hotspur	42	17	9	16	54	55	43
12	Arsenal	42	12	18	12	51	49	42
13	Wolverhampton W.	42	12	16	14	55	57	40
14	Burnley	42	12	15	15	56	61	39
15	Nottingham Forest	42	10	18	14	50	71	38
16	West Bromwich Albion	42	14	9	19	58	66	37
17	West Ham United	42	12	12	18	51	60	36
18	Ipswich Town	42	10	11	21	40	63	31
19	Southampton	42	6	17	19	46	67	29
20	Crystal Palace	42	6	15	21	34	68	27
21	Sunderland	42	6	14	22	30	68	26
22	Sheffield Wednesday	42	8	9	25	40	71	25

SQUAD: Colin Boulton, Barry Butlin, Willie Carlin, Peter Daniel, Alan Durban, Les Green, Kevin Hector, Tony Hennessey, Alan Hinton, Dave Mackay, Roy McFarland, John McGovern, John O'Hare, Tony Rhodes, John Richardson, John Robson, Arthur Stewart, Jim Walker, Ron Webster, Frank Wignall.

1970-71

Sat 15 Aug 1970	Chelsea	A	League	L 1-2
Wed 19 Aug 1970	Wolverhampton Wanderers	A	League	W 4-2
Sat 22 Aug 1970	Stoke City	H	League	W 2-0
Wed 26 Aug 1970	Ipswich Town	H	League	W 2-0
Sat 29 Aug 1970	Huddersfield Town	A	League	D 0-0
Wed 02 Sep 1970	Coventry City	H	League	L 3-4
Sat 05 Sep 1970	Newcastle United	H	League	L 1-2
Tues 08 Sep 1970	Halifax Town	H	LC 2	W 3-1
Sat 12 Sep 1970	Southampton	A	League	L 0-4
Sat 19 Sep 1970	Burnley	H	League	W 1-0
Sat 26 Sep 1970	West Bromwich Albion	A	League	L 1-2
Sat 03 Oct 1970	Tottenham Hotspur	H	League	D 1-1
Tues 07 Oct 1970	Millwall	H	LC 3	W 4-2
Sat 10 Oct 1970	Everton	A	League	D 1-1
Sat 17 Oct 1970	Chelsea	H	League	L 1-2
Sat 24 Oct 1970	Leeds United	H	League	L 0-2
Tues 27 Oct 1970	Coventry City	A	LC 4	L 0-1
Sat 31 Oct 1970	Arsenal	A	League	L 0-2
Sat 07 Nov 1970	Liverpool	H	League	D 0-0
Sat 14 Nov 1970	Manchester City	A	League	D 1-1
Sat 21 Nov 1970	Blackpool	H	League	W 2-0
Sat 28 Nov 1970	Nottingham Forest	A	League	W 4-2
Sat 05 Dec 1970	West Ham United	H	League	L 2-4
Sat 12 Dec 1970	Crystal Palace	A	League	D 0-0
Sat 19 Dec 1970	Stoke City	A	League	L 0-1
Sat 26 Dec 1970	Manchester United	H	League	D 4-4
Sat 02 Jan 1971	Chester City	A	FAC 3	W 0-1
Sat 09 Jan 1971	Wolverhampton Wanderers	H	League	L 1-2
Sat 16 Jan 1971	Ipswich Town	A	League	W 1-0
Sat 23 Jan 1971	Wolverhampton Wanderers	H	FAC 4	W 2-1
Sat 06 Feb 1971	West Ham United	A	League	W 4-1
Sat 13 Feb 1971	Everton	A	FAC 5	L 0-1
Wed 17 Feb 1971	Crystal Palace	H	League	W 1-0
Sat 20 Feb 1971	Blackpool	A	League	W 1-0
Sat 27 Feb 1971	Arsenal	H	League	W 2-0
Sat 06 Mar 1971	Leeds United	A	League	L 0-1
Sat 13 Mar 1971	Manchester City	H	League	D 0-0
Sat 20 Mar 1971	Liverpool	A	League	L 0-2
Sat 27 Mar 1971	Newcastle United	A	League	L 1-3
Wed 31 Mar 1971	Nottingham Forest	H	League	L 1-2
Sat 03 Apr 1971	Huddersfield Town	H	League	W 3-2

Wed 07 Apr 1971	Tottenham Hotspur	A	League	L 1-2
Sat 10 Apr 1971	Manchester United	A	League	W 2-1
Mon 12 Apr 1971	Southampton	H	League	D 0-0
Sat 17 Apr 1971	Everton	H	League	W 3-1
Sat 24 Apr 1971	Burnley	A	League	W 2-1
Tue 27 Apr 1971	Coventry City	A	League	D 0-0
Sat 01 May 1971	West Bromwich Albion	H	League	W 2-0

DIVISION ONE

1	Arsenal	42	29	7	6	71	29	65
2	Leeds United	42	27	10	5	72	30	64
3	Tottenham Hotspur	42	19	14	9	54	33	52
4	Wolverhampton W.	42	22	8	12	64	54	52
5	Liverpool	42	17	17	8	42	24	51
6	Chelsea	42	18	15	9	52	42	51
7	Southampton	42	17	12	13	56	44	46
8	Manchester United	42	16	11	15	65	66	43
9	Derby County	42	16	10	16	56	54	42
10	Coventry City	42	16	10	16	37	38	42
11	Manchester City	42	12	17	13	47	42	41
12	Newcastle United	42	14	13	15	44	46	41
13	Stoke City	42	12	13	17	44	48	37
14	Everton	42	12	13	17	54	60	37
15	Huddersfield Town	42	11	14	17	40	49	36
16	Nottingham Forest	42	14	8	20	42	61	36
17	West Bromwich Albion	42	10	15	17	58	75	35
18	Crystal Palace	42	12	11	19	39	57	35
19	Ipswich Town	42	12	10	20	42	48	34
20	West Ham United	42	10	14	18	47	60	34
21	Burnley	42	7	13	22	29	63	27
22	Blackpool	42	4	15	23	34	66	23

SQUAD: Colin Boulton, Jeff Bourne, Barry Butlin, Willie Carlin, Peter Daniel, Alan Durban, Archie Gemmill, Les Green, Kevin Hector, Tony Hennessey, Alan Hinton, Dave Mackay, Roy McFarland, John McGovern, John O'Hare, Tony Rhodes, John Richardson, John Robson, Colin Todd, Jim Walker, Ron Webster, Frank Wignall,

1971-72

Sat 14 Aug 1971	Manchester United	H	League	D 2-2
Wed 18 Aug 1971	West Ham United	H	League	W 2-0
Sat 21 Aug 1971	Leicester City	A	League	W 2-0
Tue 24 Aug 1971	Coventry City	A	League	D 2-2
Sat 28 Aug 1971	Southampton	H	League	D 2-2
Tue 31 Aug 1971	Ipswich Town	A	League	D 0-0
Sat 04 Sep 1971	Everton	A	League	W 2-0
Wed 08 Sep 1971	Leeds United	H	LC 2	D 0-0
Sat 11 Sep 1971	Stoke City	H	League	W 4-0
Sat 18 Sep 1971	Chelsea	A	League	D 1-1
Sat 25 Sep 1971	West Bromwich Albion	H	League	D 0-0
Sat 27 Sep 1971	Leeds United	A	LC 2 R	L 0-2
Sat 02 Oct 1971	Newcastle United	A	League	W 1-0
Sat 09 Oct 1971	Tottenham Hotspur	H	League	D 2-2
Sat 16 Oct 1971	Manchester United	A	League	L 0-1
Sat 23 Oct 1971	Arsenal	H	League	W 2-1
Sat 30 Oct 1971	Nottingham Forest	A	League	W 2-0
Sat 06 Nov 1971	Crystal Palace	H	League	W 3-0
Sat 13 Nov 1971	Wolverhampton Wanderers	A	League	L 1-2
Sat 20 Nov 1971	Sheffield United	H	League	W 3-0
Sat 27 Nov 1971	Huddersfield Town	A	League	L 1-2
Sat 04 Dec 1971	Manchester City	H	League	W 3-1
Sat 11 Dec 1971	Liverpool	A	League	L 2-3
Sat 18 Dec 1971	Everton	H	League	W 2-0
Mon 27 Dec 1971	Leeds United	A	League	L 0-3
Sat 01 Jan 1972	Chelsea	H	League	W 1-0
Sat 08 Jan 1972	Southampton	A	League	W 2-1
Sat 15 Jan 1972	Shrewsbury Town	H	FAC 3	W 2-0
Sat 22 Jan 1972	West Ham United	A	League	D 3-3
Sat 29 Jan 1972	Coventry City	H	League	W 1-0
Sat 05 Feb 1972	Notts County	H	FAC 4	W 6-0
Sat 12 Feb 1972	Arsenal	A	League	L 0-2
Sat 19 Feb 1972	Nottingham Forest	H	League	W 4-0
Sat 29 Feb 1972	Arsenal	A	FAC 5	D 0-0
Sat 04 Mar 1972	Wolverhampton Wanderers	H	League	W 2-1
Sat 11 Mar 1972	Tottenham Hotspur	A	League	W 1-0
Mon 13 Mar 1972	Arsenal	H	FAC 5 R	L 0-1
Sat 18 Mar 1972	Leicester City	H	League	W 3-0
Wed 22 Mar 1972	Ipswich Town	H	League	W 1-0
Sat 25 Mar 1972	Stoke City	A	League	D 1-1

Tue 28 Mar 1972	Crystal Palace	A	League	W 1-0
Sat 01 Apr 1972	Leeds United	H	League	W 2-0
Mon 03 Apr 1972	Newcastle United	H	League	L 0-1
Wed 05 Apr 1972	West Bromwich Albion	A	League	D 0-0
Sat 08 Apr 1972	Sheffield United	A	League	W 4-0
Sat 15 Apr 1972	Huddersfield Town	H	League	W 3-0
Sat 22 Apr 1972	Manchester City	A	League	L 0-2
Mon 01 May 1972	Liverpool	H	League	W 1-0

DIVISION ONE

1	Derby County	42	24	10	8	69	33	58
2	Leeds United	42	24	9	9	73	31	57
3	Liverpool	42	24	9	9	64	30	57
4	Manchester City	42	23	11	8	77	45	57
5	Arsenal	42	22	8	12	58	40	52
6	Tottenham Hotspur	42	19	13	10	63	42	51
7	Chelsea	42	18	12	12	58	49	48
8	Manchester United	42	19	10	13	69	61	48
9	Wolverhampton W.	42	18	11	13	65	57	47
10	Sheffield United	42	17	12	13	61	60	46
11	Newcastle United	42	15	11	16	49	52	41
12	Leicester City	42	13	13	16	41	46	39
13	Ipswich Town	42	11	16	15	39	53	38
14	West Ham United	42	12	12	18	47	51	36
15	Everton	42	9	18	15	37	48	36
16	West Bromwich Albion	42	12	11	19	42	54	35
17	Stoke City	42	10	15	17	39	56	35
18	Coventry City	42	9	15	18	44	67	33
19	Southampton	42	12	7	23	52	80	31
20	Crystal Palace	42	8	13	21	39	65	29
21	Nottingham Forest	42	8	9	25	47	81	25
22	Huddersfield Town	42	6	13	23	27	59	25

SQUAD: Tony Bailey, Colin Boulton, Jeff Bourne, Barry Butlin, Peter Daniel, Roger Davies, Alan Durban, Archie Gemmill, Kevin Hector, Tony Hennessey, Alan Hinton, Dave Mackay, Roy McFarland, John McGovern, John O'Hare, Steve Powell, John Robson, Colin Todd, Jim Walker, Ron Webster, Frank Wignall.

1972-73

Sat 12 Aug 1972	Southampton	A	League	D 1-1
Tue 15 Aug 1972	Crystal Palace	A	League	D 0-0
Sat 19 Aug 1972	Chelsea	H	League	L 1-2
Wed 23 Aug 1972	Manchester City	H	League	W 1-0
Sat 26 Aug 1972	Norwich City	A	League	L 0-1
Tue 29 Aug 1972	Everton	A	League	L 0-1
Sat 02 Sep 1972	Liverpool	H	League	W 2-1
Tues 05 Sep 1972	Swindon Town	A	LC 2	W 1-0
Sat 09 Sep 1972	West Bromwich Albion	A	League	L 1-2
Wed 13 Sep 1972	Željeznicar	H	EC 1 1L	W 2-0
Sat 16 Sep 1972	Birmingham City	H	League	W 1-0
Sat 23 Sep 1972	Manchester United	A	League	L 0-3
Wed 27 Sep 1972	Željeznicar	A	EC 1 2L	W 2-1
Sat 30 Sep 1972	Tottenham Hotspur	H	League	W 2-1
Wed 04 Oct 1972	Chelsea	H	LC 3	D 0-0
Sat 07 Oct 1972	Leeds United	A	League	L 0-5
Mon 09 Oct 1972	Chelsea	A	LC 3 R	L 0-1
Sat 14 Oct 1972	Leicester City	H	League	W 2-1
Sat 21 Oct 1972	Ipswich Town	A	League	L 1-3
Wed 25 Oct 1972	Benfica	H	EC 2 1L	W 3-0
Sat 28 Oct 1972	Sheffield United	H	League	W 2-1
Sat 04 Nov 1972	Manchester City	A	League	L 0-4
Wed 08 Nov 1972	Benfica	A	EC 2 2L	D 0-0
Sat 11 Nov 1972	Crystal Palace	H	League	D 2-2
Sat 18 Nov 1972	West Ham United	A	League	W 2-1
Sat 25 Nov 1972	Arsenal	H	League	W 5-0
Sat 02 Dec 1972	Wolverhampton Wanderers	A	League	W 2-1
Sat 09 Dec 1972	Coventry City	H	League	W 2-0
Sat 16 Dec 1972	Newcastle United	H	League	D 1-1
Sat 23 Dec 1972	Stoke City	A	League	L 0-4
Tue 26 Dec 1972	Manchester United	H	League	W 3-1
Sat 30 Dec 1972	Chelsea	A	League	D 1-1
Sat 06 Jan 1973	Norwich City	H	League	W 1-0
Sat 13 Jan 1973	Peterborough	A	FAC 3	W 1-0
Sat 20 Jan 1973	Liverpool	A	League	D 1-1
Sat 27 Jan 1973	West Bromwich Albion	H	League	W 2-0
Sat 03 Feb 1973	Tottenham Hotspur	H	FAC 4	D 1-1
Wed 07 Feb 1973	Tottenham Hotspur	A	FAC 4 R	W 5-3
Sat 10 Feb 1973	Birmingham City	A	League	L 0-2
Wed 14 Feb 1973	Stoke City	H	League	L 0-3
Sat 17 Feb 1973	Southampton	H	League	W 4-0
Sat 24 Feb 1973	QPR	H	FAC 5	W 4-2

Wed 28 Feb 1973	Newcastle United	A	League	L 0-2
Sat 03 Mar 1973	Leeds United	H	League	L 2-3
Wed 7 Mar 1973	Spartak Trnava	A	EC QF 1L	L 0-1
Sat 10 Mar 1973	Leicester City	A	League	D 0-0
Sat 17 Mar 1973	Leeds United	H	FAC 6	L 0-1
Sat 21 Mar 1973	Spartak Trnava	H	EC QF 2L	W 2-0
Sat 24 Mar 1973	Sheffield United	A	League	L 1-3
Sat 31 Mar 1973	Arsenal	A	League	W 1-0
Wed 11 Apr 1973	Juventus	A	EC SF 1L	L 1-3
Sat 14 Apr 1973	Coventry City	A	League	W 2-0
Wed 18 Apr 1973	Tottenham Hotspur	A	League	L 0-1
Sat 21 Apr 1973	West Ham United	H	League	D 1-1
Wed 25 Apr 1973	Juventus	H	EC SF 2L	D 0-0
Sat 28 Apr 1973	Everton	H	League	W 3-1
Mon 30 Apr 1973	Ipswich Town	H	League	W 3-0
Fri 04 May 1973	Wolverhampton Wanderers	H	League	W 3-0

DIVISION ONE

1	Liverpool	42	25	10	7	72	42	60
2	Arsenal	42	23	11	8	57	43	57
3	Leeds United	42	21	11	10	71	45	53
4	Ipswich Town	42	17	14	11	55	45	48
5	Wolverhampton W.	42	18	11	13	66	54	47
6	West Ham United	42	17	12	13	67	53	46
7	Derby County	42	19	8	15	56	54	46
8	Tottenham Hotspur	42	16	13	13	58	48	45
9	Newcastle United	42	16	13	13	60	51	45
10	Birmingham City	42	15	12	15	53	54	42
11	Manchester City	42	15	11	16	57	60	41
12	Chelsea	42	13	14	15	49	51	40
13	Southampton	42	11	18	13	47	52	40
14	Sheffield United	42	15	10	17	51	59	40
15	Stoke City	42	14	10	18	61	56	38
16	Leicester City	42	10	17	15	40	46	37
17	Everton	42	13	11	18	41	49	37
18	Manchester United	42	12	13	17	44	60	37
19	Coventry City	42	13	9	20	40	55	35
20	Norwich City	42	11	10	21	36	63	32
21	Crystal Palace	42	9	12	21	41	58	30
22	West Bromwich Albion	42	9	10	23	38	62	28

SQUAD: Colin Boulton, Jeff Bourne, Barry Butlin, Peter Daniel, Roger Davies, Alan Durban, Archie Gemmill, Kevin Hector, Tony Hennessey, Alan Hinton, Alan Lewis, Roy McFarland, John McGovern, Graham Moseley, David Nish, John O'Hare, Tony Parry, Steve Powell, John Robson, John Sims, Colin Todd, Jim Walker, Ron Webster

1973-74

Sat 25 Aug 1973	Chelsea	H	League	W 1-0
Wed 29 Aug 1973	Manchester City	H	League	W 1-0
Sat 01 Sep 1973	Birmingham City	A	League	D 0-0
Tue 04 Sep 1973	Liverpool	A	League	L 0-2
Sat 08 Sep 1973	Everton	H	League	W 2-1
Wed 12 Sep 1973	Liverpool	H	League	W 3-1
Sat 15 Sep 1973	Burnley	A	League	D 1-1
Tue 18 Sep 1973	Coventry City	A	League	L 0-1
Sat 22 Sep 1973	Southampton	H	League	W 6-2
Sat 29 Sep 1973	Tottenham Hotspur	A	League	L 0-1
Sat 06 Oct 1973	Norwich City	H	League	D 1-1
Mon 08 Oct 1973	Sunderland	H	League Cup	D 2-2
Sat 13 Oct 1973	Manchester United	A	League	W 1-0

DIVISION ONE - as of 15/10/1973

1	Leeds United	11	8	3	0	23	7	19
2	Burnley	11	7	3	1	21	11	17
3	Derby County	12	6	3	3	16	10	15
4	Coventry City	12	6	3	3	14	9	15
5	Everton	11	5	4	2	13	9	14
6	Newcastle United	11	5	3	3	18	13	13
7	Liverpool	11	5	3	3	12	10	13
8	Leicester City	11	3	7	1	13	11	13
9	Sheffield United	11	5	2	4	14	13	12
10	Ipswich Town	11	4	4	3	18	19	12
11	Arsenal	11	5	1	5	13	14	11
12	Manchester City	11	4	3	4	13	14	11
13	Southampton	11	4	3	4	14	17	11
14	Queens Park Rangers	11	2	6	3	15	16	10
15	Tottenham Hotspur	11	4	2	5	13	15	10
16	Chelsea	11	3	2	6	16	17	8
17	Stoke City	11	1	6	4	11	13	8
18	Manchester United	11	3	2	6	9	13	8
19	Wolverhampton W.	11	3	2	6	13	19	8
20	Norwich City	11	1	5	5	9	16	7
21	Birmingham City	11	1	3	7	10	23	5
22	West Ham United	11	0	4	7	10	19	4

SQUAD: Colin Boulton, Jeff Bourne, Peter Daniel, Roger Davies, Archie Gemmill, Kevin Hector, Alan Hinton, Roy McFarland, John McGovern, Graham Moseley, Harry Newton, David Nish, John O'Hare, Steve Powell, Bruce Rioch, Rod Thomas, Colin Todd, Jim Walker, Ron Webster.

BRIGHTON

1973-74

Sat 03 Nov 1973	York City	H	League	D 0-0
Sat 10 Nov 1973	Huddersfield Town	A	League	D 2-2
Tue 13 Nov 1973	Walsall	A	League	W 1-0
Sat 17 Nov 1973	Chesterfield	H	League	D 0-0
Sat 24 Nov 1973	Walton & Hersham	A	FAC 1	D 0-0
Sat 28 Nov 1973	Walton & Hersham	H	FAC 1 R	L 0-4
Sat 01 Dec 1973	Bristol Rovers	H	League	L 2-8
Sat 08 Dec 1973	Tranmere Rovers	A	League	L 1-4
Sat 22 Dec 1973	Watford	A	League	L 0-1
Wed 26 Dec 1973	Aldershot	H	League	L 0-1
Sat 29 Dec 1973	Plymouth Argyle	H	League	W 1-0
Tue 01 Jan 1974	AFC Bournemouth	A	League	D 0-0
Sat 12 Jan 1974	Charlton Athletic	A	League	W 4-0
Sun 20 Jan 1974	Rochdale	H	League	W 2-1
Sun 27 Jan 1974	Cambridge United	A	League	D 1-1
Sat 02 Feb 1974	Port Vale	A	League	L 1-2
Sat 09 Feb 1974	Grimsby Town	H	League	D 1-1
Sat 16 Feb 1974	Halifax Town	A	League	D 2-2
Sat 23 Feb 1974	Blackburn Rovers	H	League	W 3-0
Wed 27 Feb 1974	Wrexham	H	League	W 2-1
Sun 03 Mar 1974	Aldershot	A	League	W 1-0
Sun 10 Mar 1974	Hereford United	H	League	W 2-1
Sat 16 Mar 1974	Shrewsbury Town	A	League	L 0-1
Wed 20 Mar 1974	Port Vale	H	League	W 2-1
Sat 23 Mar 1974	Huddersfield Town	H	League	L 1-2
Mon 25 Mar 1974	Wrexham	A	League	L 0-1
Sat 30 Mar 1974	York City	A	League	L 0-3
Wed 03 Apr 1974	Cambridge United	H	League	W 4-1
Sat 06 Apr 1974	Walsall	H	League	W 2-1
Fri 12 Apr 1974	Southend United	A	League	W 2-0
Sat 13 Apr 1974	Chesterfield	A	League	L 0-1
Mon 15 Apr 1974	Southend United	H	League	L 0-2
Sat 20 Apr 1974	Tranmere Rovers	H	League	L 1-3
Sat 27 Apr 1974	Bristol Rovers	A	League	D 1-1

DIVISION THREE

1	Oldham Athletic	46	25	12	9	83	47	62
2	Bristol Rovers	46	22	17	7	65	33	61
3	York City	46	21	19	6	67	38	61
4	Wrexham	46	22	12	12	63	43	56
5	Chesterfield	46	21	14	11	55	42	56
6	Grimsby Town	46	18	15	13	67	50	51
7	Watford	46	19	12	15	64	56	50
8	Aldershot	46	19	11	16	65	52	49
9	Halifax Town	46	14	21	11	48	51	49
10	Huddersfield Town	46	17	13	16	56	55	47
11	Bournemouth	46	16	15	15	54	58	47
12	Southend United	46	16	14	16	62	62	46
13	Blackburn Rovers	46	18	10	18	62	64	46
14	Charlton Athletic	46	19	8	19	66	73	46
15	Walsall	46	16	13	17	57	48	45
16	Tranmere Rovers	46	15	15	16	50	44	45
17	Plymouth Argyle	46	17	10	19	59	54	44
18	Hereford United	46	14	15	17	53	57	43
19	Brighton & Hove Albion	46	16	11	19	52	58	43
20	Port Vale	46	14	14	18	52	58	42
21	Cambridge United	46	13	9	24	48	81	35
22	Shrewsbury Town	46	10	11	25	41	62	31
23	Southport	46	6	16	24	35	82	28
24	Rochdale	46	2	17	27	38	94	21

SQUAD: Ken Beamish, John Boyle, Barry Bridges, Brian Bromley, Michael Brown, Dave Busby, Mike Conway, Peter Downsborough, Paul Fuschillo, Norman Gall, Ken Goodeve, Ian Goodwin, Peter Grummitt, Pat Hilton, Ron Howell, Graham Howell, George Ley, Billy McEwan, Bert Murray, Peter O'Sullivan, Steve Piper, Brian Powney, Lammie Robertson, Eddie Spearritt, John Templeman, Tony Towner, Ron Welch, Harry Wilson.

Leeds United

1974-75

Sat 17 Aug 1974	Stoke City	A	League	L 0-3
Wed 21 Aug 1974	Queens Park Rangers	H	League	L 0-1
Sat 24 Aug 1974	Birmingham City	H	League	W 1-0
Tue 27 Aug 1974	Queens Park Rangers	A	League	D 1-1
Sat 31 Aug 1974	Manchester City	A	League	L 1-2
Sat 07 Sep 1974	Luton Town	H	League	D 1-1
Wed 11 Sep 1974	Huddersfield Town	A	LC 2	D 1-1

DIVISION ONE - as of 12th September 1974

1	Liverpool	6	5	1	0	14	4	11
2	Ipswich Town	6	5	0	1	9	3	10
3	Manchester City	6	4	1	1	11	8	9
4	Stoke City	6	3	2	1	9	4	8
5	Everton	6	3	2	1	8	6	8
6	Sheffield United	6	3	2	1	10	8	8
7	Carlisle United	6	3	1	2	6	4	7
8	Middlesbrough	6	2	3	1	7	5	7
9	Wolverhampton W'drs.	6	2	3	1	8	7	7
10	Newcastle United	6	2	2	2	12	12	6
11	Derby County	6	1	4	1	6	6	6
12	Chelsea	6	2	2	2	9	11	6
13	Burnley	6	2	1	3	9	9	5
14	Leicester City	6	1	3	2	8	9	5
15	Queens Park Rangers	6	1	3	2	4	5	5
16	Arsenal	6	2	0	4	6	7	4
17	Birmingham City	6	1	2	3	6	10	4
18	Luton Town	6	0	4	2	4	7	4
19	Leeds United	6	1	2	3	4	8	4
20	Coventry City	6	0	3	3	7	13	3
21	West Ham United	6	1	1	4	5	11	3
22	Tottenham Hotspur	6	1	0	5	5	10	2

SQUAD: Mick Bates, Billy Bremner, Trevor Cherry, Allan Clarke, Terry Cooper, Johnny Giles, Frank Gray, Eddie Gray, Peter Hampton, Carl Harris, David Harvey, Norman Hunter, Joe Jordan, Glan Letheran, Gary Liddell, Peter Lorimer, Paul Madeley, John McGovern, Duncan McKenzie, Gordon McQueen, John O'Hare, Paul Reaney, Byron Stevenson, Dave Stewart, Gwyn Thomas, Terry Yorath.

NOTTINGHAM FOREST

1974-75

Wed 08 Jan 1975	Tottenham H	A	FAC 3 R	W 1-0
Sat 11 Jan 1975	Fulham	A	League	W 1-0
Sat 18 Jan 1975	Orient	H	League	D 2-2
Sat 28 Jan 1975	Fulham	A	FAC 4	D 0-0
Sat 01 Feb 1975	Oldham Athletic	A	League	L 0-2
Mon 03 Feb 1975	Fulham	H	FAC 4 R	D 1-1
Wed 05 Feb 1975	Fulham	A	FAC 4 2R	D 1-1
Sat 08 Feb 1975	Bolton Wanderers	H	League	L 2-3
Mon 10 Feb 1975	Fulham	H	FAC 4 3R	L 1-2
Fri 14 Feb 1975	York City	A	League	D 1-1
Sat 22 Feb 1975	Cardiff City	H	League	D 0-0
Fri 28 Feb 1975	Oxford United	A	League	D 1-1
Sat 08 Mar 1975	Aston Villa	H	League	L 2-3
Sat 15 Mar 1975	Sunderland	A	League	D 0-0
Sat 22 Mar 1975	Manchester United	H	League	L 0-1
Tue 25 Mar 1975	Notts. County	A	League	D 2-2
Sat 29 Mar 1975	Blackpool	A	League	D 0-0
Tue 01 Apr 1975	Sheffield Wednesday	H	League	W 1-0
Sat 05 Apr 1975	Bristol Rovers	A	League	L 2-4
Sat 12 Apr 1975	Southampton	H	League	D 0-0
Sat 19 Apr 1975	Norwich City	A	League	L 0-3
Sat 26 Apr 1975	West Bromwich Albion	H	League	W 2-1

DIVISION TWO

1	Manchester United	42	26	9	7	66	30	61
2	Aston Villa	42	25	8	9	79	32	58
3	Norwich City	42	20	13	9	58	37	53
4	Sunderland	42	19	13	10	65	35	51
5	Bristol City	42	21	8	13	47	33	50
6	West Bromwich Albion	42	18	9	15	54	42	45
7	Blackpool	42	14	17	11	38	33	45
8	Hull City	42	15	14	13	40	53	44
9	Fulham	42	13	16	13	44	39	42
10	Bolton Wanderers	42	15	12	15	45	41	42
11	Oxford United	42	15	12	15	41	51	42
12	Orient	42	11	20	11	28	39	42
13	Southampton	42	15	11	16	53	54	41
14	Notts County	42	12	16	14	49	59	40
15	York City	42	14	10	18	51	55	38
16	Nottingham Forest	42	12	14	16	43	55	38
17	Portsmouth	42	12	13	17	44	54	37
18	Oldham Athletic	42	10	15	17	40	48	35
19	Bristol Rovers	42	12	11	19	42	64	35
20	Millwall	42	10	12	20	44	56	32
21	Cardiff City	42	9	14	19	36	62	32
22	Sheffield Wednesday	42	5	11	26	29	64	21

SQUAD: Viv Anderson, Ian Bowyer, Barry Butlin, Sammy Chapman, John Cottam, Miah Dennehy, John Galley, Paddy Greenwood, Tommy Jackson, David Jones, George Lyall, Neil Martin, Jim McCann, John McGovern, Jim Mcintosh, John Middleton, John O'Hare, Liam O'Kane, Martin O'Neill, Dennis Peacock, Paul Richardson, John Robertson, Dave Serella, Tony Woodcock.

1975/76

Sat 16 Aug 1975	Plymouth Argyle	H	League	W 2-0
Tues 19 Aug 1975	Rotherham United	A	LC 1 1L	W 2-1
Sat 23 Aug 1975	Portsmouth	A	League	D 1-1
Wed 27 Aug 1975	Rotherham United	H	LC1 2L	W 5-1
Sat 30 Aug 1975	Notts. County	H	League	L 0-1
Sat 06 Sep 1975	Chelsea	A	League	D 0-0
Wed 10 Sep 1975	Plymouth Argyle	H	LC 2	W 1-0
Sat 13 Sep 1975	Hull City	H	League	L 1-2
Sat 20 Sep 1975	Oxford United	A	League	W 1-0
Wed 24 Sep 1975	Charlton Athletic	H	League	L 1-2
Sat 27 Sep 1975	Bolton Wanderers	H	League	L 1-2
Sat 04 Oct 1975	Bristol Rovers	A	League	L 2-4
Wed 08 Oct 1975	Manchester City	A	LC 3	L 1-2
Sat 11 Oct 1975	Fulham	A	League	D 0-0
Sat 18 Oct 1975	Southampton	H	League	W 3-1
Tue 21 Oct 1975	Luton Town	H	League	D 0-0
Sat 25 Oct 1975	Oldham Athletic	A	League	D 0-0
Sat 01 Nov 1975	Carlisle United	H	League	W 4-0
Tue 04 Nov 1975	Blackpool	A	League	D 1-1
Sat 08 Nov 1975	Sunderland	A	League	L 0-3
Sat 15 Nov 1975	Bristol City	H	League	W 1-0
Sat 22 Nov 1975	Southampton	A	League	W 3-0
Sat 29 Nov 1975	York City	H	League	W 1-0
Sat 06 Dec 1975	Orient	A	League	D 1-1
Sat 13 Dec 1975	Portsmouth	H	League	L 0-1
Sat 20 Dec 1975	Plymouth Argyle	A	League	L 0-1
Fri 26 Dec 1975	West Bromwich Albion	H	League	L 0-2
Sat 27 Dec 1975	Blackburn Rovers	A	League	W 4-1
Sat 03 jan 1976	Peterborough	H	FAC 3	D 0-0
Wed 07 Jan 1976	Peterborough	A	FAC 3 R	L 0-1
Sat 10 Jan 1976	Hull City	A	League	L 0-1
Sat 17 Jan 1976	Chelsea	H	League	L 1-3
Sat 31 Jan 1976	Luton Town	A	League	D 1-1
Sat 07 Feb 1976	Blackpool	H	League	W 3-0
Sat 21 Feb 1976	Bristol City	A	League	W 2-0
Tue 24 Feb 1976	Charlton Athletic	A	League	D 2-2
Sat 28 Feb 1976	Oldham Athletic	H	League	W 4-3
Sat 06 Mar 1976	Carlisle United	A	League	D 1-1
Sat 13 Mar 1976	Fulham	H	League	W 1-0
Wed 17 Mar 1976	Sunderland	H	League	W 2-1
Sat 20 Mar 1976	York City	A	League	L 2-3

Sat 27 Mar 1976	Orient	H	League	W 1-0
Sat 03 Apr 1976	Bolton Wanderers	A	League	D 0-0
Sat 10 Apr 1976	Oxford United	H	League	W 4-0
Tue 13 Apr 1976	Notts. County	A	League	D 0-0
Sat 17 Apr 1976	West Bromwich Albion	A	League	L 0-2
Tue 20 Apr 1976	Blackburn Rovers	H	League	W 1-0
Sat 24 Apr 1976	Bristol Rovers	H	League	W 3-0

DIVISION TWO

1	Sunderland	42	24	8	10	67	36	56
2	Bristol City	42	19	15	8	59	35	53
3	West Bromwich Albion	42	20	13	9	50	33	53
4	Bolton Wanderers	42	20	12	10	64	38	52
5	Notts County	42	19	11	12	60	41	49
6	Southampton	42	21	7	14	66	50	49
7	Luton Town	42	19	10	13	61	51	48
8	Nottingham Forest	42	17	12	13	55	40	46
9	Charlton Athletic	42	15	12	15	61	72	42
10	Blackpool	42	14	14	14	40	49	42
11	Chelsea	42	12	16	14	53	54	40
12	Fulham	42	13	14	15	45	47	40
13	Orient	42	13	14	15	37	39	40
14	Hull City	42	14	11	17	45	49	39
15	Blackburn Rovers	42	12	14	16	45	50	38
16	Plymouth Argyle	42	13	12	17	48	54	38
17	Oldham Athletic	42	13	12	17	57	68	38
18	Bristol Rovers	42	11	16	15	38	50	38
19	Carlisle United	42	12	13	17	45	59	37
20	Oxford United	42	11	11	20	39	59	33
21	York City	42	10	8	24	39	71	28
22	Portsmouth	42	9	7	26	32	61	25

SQUAD: Viv Anderson, Colin Barrett, Bert Bowery, Ian Bowyer, Barry Butlin, Sammy Chapman, Frank Clark, John Cottam, Terry Curran, Bryn Gunn, George Lyall, Jim McCann, John McGovern, Jim Mcintosh, John Middleton, John O'Hare, Liam O'Kane, Martin O'Neill, Paul Richardson, John Robertson, Dave Sunley, Peter Wells, Tony Woodcock,

1976/77

Sat 21 Aug 1976	Fulham	A	League	D 2-2
Wed 25 Aug 1976	Charlton Athletic	H	League	D 1-1
Sat 28 Aug 1976	Wolverhampton Wanderers	H	League	L 1-3
Tues 31 Aug 1976	Walsall	A	LC 2	W 4-2
Sat 04 Sep 1976	Luton Town	A	League	D 1-1
Sat 11 Sep 1976	Hereford United	H	League	W 4-3
Sat 18 Sep 1976	Southampton	A	League	D 1-1
Tues 21 Sep 1976	Coventry City	H	LC 4	L 0-3
Sat 25 Sep 1976	Carlisle United	H	League	W 5-1
Sat 02 Oct 1976	Hull City	A	League	L 0-1
Sat 09 Oct 1976	Sheffield United	H	League	W 6-1
Sat 16 Oct 1976	Blackpool	A	League	L 0-1
Sat 23 Oct 1976	Burnley	H	League	W 5-2
Sat 30 Oct 1976	Oldham Athletic	A	League	L 0-1
Sat 06 Nov 1976	Blackburn Rovers	H	League	W 3-0
Sat 13 Nov 1976	Orient	A	League	W 1-0
Sat 20 Nov 1976	Chelsea	H	League	D 1-1
Sat 27 Nov 1976	Cardiff City	A	League	W 3-0
Sat 04 Dec 1976	Bristol Rovers	H	League	W 4-2
Sat 11 Dec 1976	Millwall	A	League	W 2-0
Sat 18 Dec 1976	Plymouth Argyle	H	League	D 1-1
Mon 27 Dec 1976	Bolton Wanderers	A	League	D 1-1
Sat 01 Jan 1977	Blackburn Rovers	A	League	W 3-1
Sat 08 Jan 1977	Bristol Rovers	H	FAC 3	D 1-1
Tues 11 Jan 1977	Bristol Rovers	A	FAC 3 R	D 1-1
Fri 14 Jan 1977	Charlton Athletic	A	League	L 1-2
Tues 18 Jan 1977	Bristol Rovers	H	FAC 3 2R	W 6-0
Sat 22 Jan 1977	Fulham	H	League	W 3-0
Sat 29 Jan 1977	Southampton	H	FAC 4	D 3-3
Tues 01 Feb 1977	Southampton	A	FAC 4 R	L 1-2
Sat 05 Feb 1977	Wolverhampton Wanderers	A	League	L 1-2
Sat 12 Feb 1977	Luton Town	H	League	L 1-2
Wed 02 Mar 1977	Hereford United	A	League	W 1-0
Sat 05 Mar 1977	Carlisle United	A	League	D 1-1
Tue 08 Mar 1977	Notts. County	H	League	L 1-2
Sat 12 Mar 1977	Hull City	H	League	W 2-0
Sat 19 Mar 1977	Sheffield United	A	League	L 0-2
Tue 22 Mar 1977	Southampton	H	League	W 2-1
Sat 26 Mar 1977	Blackpool	H	League	W 3-0
Tue 29 Mar 1977	Orient	H	League	W 3-0
Sat 02 Apr 1977	Burnley	A	League	W 1-0

Wed 06 Apr 1977	Bolton Wanderers	H	League	W 3-1
Sat 09 Apr 1977	Notts. County	A	League	D 1-1
Sat 16 Apr 1977	Chelsea	A	League	L 1-2
Sat 23 Apr 1977	Cardiff City	H	League	L 0-1
Wed 27 Apr 1977	Oldham Athletic	H	League	W 3-0
Sat 30 Apr 1977	Bristol Rovers	A	League	D 1-1
Mon 02 May 1977	Plymouth Argyle	A	League	W 2-1
Sat 07 May 1977	Millwall	H	League	W 1-0

DIVISION TWO

1	Wolverhampton W.	42	22	13	7	84	45	57
2	Chelsea	42	21	13	8	73	53	55
3	Nottingham Forest	42	21	10	11	77	43	52
4	Bolton Wanderers	42	20	11	11	75	54	51
5	Blackpool	42	17	17	8	58	42	51
6	Luton	42	21	6	15	67	48	48
7	Charlton Athletic	42	16	16	10	71	58	48
8	Notts County	42	19	10	13	65	60	48
9	Southampton	42	17	10	15	72	67	44
10	Millwall	42	15	13	14	57	53	43
11	Sheffield United	42	14	12	16	54	63	40
12	Blackburn Rovers	42	15	9	18	42	54	39
13	Oldham Athletic	42	14	10	18	52	64	38
14	Hull City	42	10	17	15	45	53	37
15	Bristol Rovers	42	12	13	17	53	68	37
16	Burnley	42	11	14	17	46	64	36
17	Fulham	42	11	13	18	54	61	35
18	Cardiff City	42	12	10	20	56	67	34
19	Orient	42	9	16	17	37	55	34
20	Carlisle United	42	11	12	19	49	75	34
21	Plymouth Argyle	42	8	16	18	46	65	32
22	Hereford United	42	8	15	19	57	78	31

SQUAD: Viv Anderson, Colin Barrett, Gary Birtles, Bert Bowery, Ian Bowyer, Barry Butlin, Sammy Chapman, Frank Clark, Terry Curran, Bryn Gunn, Sean Haslegrave, Larry Lloyd, John McGovern, John Middleton, John O'Hare, Liam O'Kane, Martin O'Neill, Paul Richardson, John Robertson, Glyn Saunders, Peter Wells, Tony Woodcock, Peter Withe, Chris Woods,

1977/78

Sat 20 Aug 1977	Everton	A	League	W 3-1
Tue 23 Aug 1977	Bristol City	H	League	W 1-0
Sat 27 Aug 1977	Derby County	H	League	W 3-0
Tues 30 Aug 1977	West Ham United	H	LC 2	W 5-0
Sat 03 Sep 1977	Arsenal	A	League	L 0-3
Sat 10 Sep 1977	Wolverhampton Wanderers	A	League	W 3-2
Sat 17 Sep 1977	Aston Villa	H	League	W 2-0
Sat 24 Sep 1977	Leicester City	A	League	W 3-0
Sat 01 Oct 1977	Norwich City	H	League	D 1-1
Tue 04 Oct 1977	Ipswich Town	H	League	W 4-0
Sat 08 Oct 1977	West Ham United	A	League	D 0-0
Sat 15 Oct 1977	Manchester City	H	League	W 2-1
Sat 22 Oct 1977	Queens Park Rangers	A	League	W 2-0
Wed 25 Oct 1977	Notts County	H	LC 3	W 4-0
Sat 29 Oct 1977	Middlesbrough	H	League	W 4-0
Sat 05 Nov 1977	Chelsea	A	League	L 0-1
Sat 12 Nov 1977	Manchester United	H	League	W 2-1
Sat 19 Nov 1977	Leeds United	A	League	L 0-1
Sat 26 Nov 1977	West Bromwich Albion	H	League	D 0-0
Tues 29 Nov 1977	Aston Villa	H	LC 4	W 4-2
Sat 03 Dec 1977	Birmingham City	A	League	W 2-0
Sat 10 Dec 1977	Coventry City	H	League	W 2-1
Sat 17 Dec 1977	Manchester United	A	League	W 4-0
Mon 26 Dec 1977	Liverpool	H	League	D 1-1
Wed 28 Dec 1977	Newcastle United	A	League	W 2-0
Sat 31 Dec 1977	Bristol City	A	League	W 3-1
Mon 02 Jan 1978	Everton	H	League	D 1-1
Sat 07 Jan 1978	Swindon Town	H	FAC 3	W 4-1
Sat 14 Jan 1978	Derby County	A	League	D 0-0
Wed 17 Jan 1978	Bury	A	LC 5	W 3-0
Sat 21 Jan 1978	Arsenal	H	League	W 2-0
Tues 31 Jan 1978	Manchester City	H	FAC 4	W 2-1
Sat 04 Feb 1978	Wolverhampton Wanderers	H	League	W 2-0
Wed 08 Feb 1978	Leeds United	A	LC SF 1L	W 3-1
Sat 18 Feb 1978	Qpr	A	FAC 5	D 1-1
Wed 22 Feb 1978	Leeds United	H	LC SF 2L	W 4-2
Sat 25 Feb 1978	Norwich City	A	League	D 3-3
Mon 27 Feb 1978	Qpr	H	FAC 5 R	D 1-1
Thurs 02 Feb 1978	Qpr	H	FAC 5 2R	W 3-1
Sat 04 Mar 1978	West Ham United	H	League	W 2-0

Sat 11 Mar 1978	Wba	A	FAC 6	L 0-2
Tue 14 Mar 1978	Leicester City	H	League	W 1-0
Sat 18 Mar 1978	Liverpool	N	LC Final	D 0-0
Wed 22 Mar 1978	Liverpool	N	LC Final R	W 1-0
Sat 25 Mar 1978	Newcastle United	H	League	W 2-0
Wed 29 Mar 1978	Middlesbrough	A	League	D 2-2
Sat 01 Apr 1978	Chelsea	H	League	W 3-1
Wed 05 Apr 1978	Aston Villa	A	League	W 1-0
Tue 11 Apr 1978	Manchester City	A	League	D 0-0
Sat 15 Apr 1978	Leeds United	H	League	D 1-1
Tue 18 Apr 1978	Queens Park Rangers	H	League	W 1-0
Sat 22 Apr 1978	Coventry City	A	League	D 0-0
Tue 25 Apr 1978	Ipswich Town	A	League	W 2-0
Sat 29 Apr 1978	Birmingham City	H	League	D 0-0
Tue 02 May 1978	West Bromwich Albion	A	League	D 2-2
Thu 04 May 1978	Liverpool	A	League	D 0-0

DIVISION ONE

1	Nottingham Forest	42	25	14	3	69	24	64
2	Liverpool	42	24	9	9	65	34	57
3	Everton	42	22	11	9	76	45	55
4	Manchester City	42	20	12	10	74	51	52
5	Arsenal	42	21	10	11	60	37	52
6	West Bromwich Albion	42	18	14	10	62	53	50
7	Coventry City	42	18	12	12	75	62	48
8	Aston Villa	42	18	10	14	57	42	46
9	Leeds United	42	18	10	14	63	53	46
10	Manchester United	42	16	10	16	67	63	42
11	Birmingham City	42	16	9	17	55	60	41
12	Derby County	42	14	13	15	54	59	41
13	Norwich City	42	11	18	13	52	66	40
14	Middlesbrough	42	12	15	15	42	54	39
15	Wolverhampton W.	42	12	12	18	51	64	36
16	Chelsea	42	11	14	17	46	69	36
17	Bristol City	42	11	13	18	49	53	35
18	Ipswich Town	42	11	13	18	47	61	35
19	Queens Park Rangers	42	9	15	18	47	64	33
20	West Ham United	42	12	8	22	52	69	32
21	Newcastle United	42	6	10	26	42	78	22
22	Leicester City	42	5	12	25	26	70	22

SQUAD: Viv Anderson, Colin Barrett, Gary Birtles, Ian Bowyer, Kenny Burns, Frank Clark, Ron Fenton, Archie Gemmill, Bryn Gunn, Larry Lloyd, John McGovern, John Middleton, Dave Needham, John O'Hare, Martin O'Neill, John Robertson, Peter Shilton, Tony Woodcock, Peter Withe, Chris Woods.

1978/79

Sat 19 Aug 1978	Tottenham Hotspur	H	League	D 1-1
Tue 22 Aug 1978	Coventry City	A	League	D 0-0
Sat 26 Aug 1978	Queens Park Rangers	A	League	D 0-0
Tues 29 Aug 1978	Oldham Athletic	A	LC 2	D 0-0
Sat 02 Sep 1978	West Bromwich Albion	H	League	D 0-0
Wed 06 Sep 1978	Oldham Athletic	H	LC 2R	W 4-2
Sat 09 Sep 1978	Arsenal	H	League	W 2-1
Wed 13 Sep 1978	Liverpool	H	EC 1R 1L	W 2-0
Sat 16 Sep 1978	Manchester United	A	League	D 1-1
Sat 23 Sep 1978	Middlesbrough	H	League	D 2-2
Wed 27 Sep 1978	Liverpool	A	EC 1R 2L	D 0-0
Sat 30 Sep 1978	Aston Villa	A	League	W 2-1
Wed 05 Oct 1978	Oxford United	A	LC 3	W 5-0
Sat 07 Oct 1978	Wolverhampton Wanderers	H	League	W 3-1
Sat 14 Oct 1978	Bristol City	A	League	W 3-1
Wed 18 Oct 1978	AEK Athens	A	EC 2R 1L	W 2-1
Sat 21 Oct 1978	Ipswich Town	H	League	W 1-0
Sat 28 Oct 1978	Southampton	A	League	D 0-0
Wed 01 Nov 1978	AEK Athens	H	EC 2R 2L	W 5-1
Sat 04 Nov 1978	Everton	H	League	D 0-0
Tues 07 Nov 1978	Everton	A	LC 4	W 3-2
Sat 11 Nov 1978	Tottenham Hotspur	A	League	W 3-1
Sat 18 Nov 1978	Queens Park Rangers	H	League	D 0-0
Sat 25 Nov 1978	Bolton Wanderers	A	League	W 1-0
Sat 09 Dec 1978	Liverpool	A	League	L 0-2
Wed 13 Dec 1978	Brighton & HA	H	LC 5	W 3-1
Sat 16 Dec 1978	Birmingham City	H	League	W 1-0
Sat 23 Dec 1978	Manchester City	A	League	D 0-0
Tue 26 Dec 1978	Derby County	H	League	D 1-1
Wed 10 Jan 1979	Aston Villa	H	FAC 3	W 2-0
Sat 13 Jan 1979	Arsenal	A	League	L 1-2
Wed 17 Jan 1979	Watford	H	LC SF 1L	W 3-1
Sat 27 jan 1979	York City	H	FAC 4	W 3-1
Tues 30 Jan 1979	Watford	A	LC SF 2L	D 0-0
Sat 03 Feb 1979	Middlesbrough	A	League	W 3-1
Sat 24 Feb 1979	Bristol City	H	League	W 2-0
Mon 26 Feb 1979	Arsenal	H	FAC 5	L 0-1
Sat 03 Mar 1979	Ipswich Town	A	League	D 1-1
Wed 07 Mar 1979	Grasshopper	H	EC QF 1L	W 4-1
Sat 10 Mar 1979	Everton	A	League	D 1-1
Wed 14 Mar 1979	Norwich City	H	League	W 2-1
Sat 17 Mar 1979	Southampton	N	LC Final	W 3-2
Wed 21 Mar 1979	Grasshopper	A	EC QF 2L	D 1-1
Sat 24 Mar 1979	Coventry City	H	League	W 3-0

Wed 28 Mar 1979	Chelsea	H	League	W 6-0
Sat 31 Mar 1979	Bolton Wanderers	H	League	D 1-1
Wed 04 Apr 1979	Aston Villa	H	League	W 4-0
Sat 07 Apr 1979	Chelsea	A	League	W 3-1
Wed 11 Apr 1979	FC Köln	H	EC SF 1L	D 3-3
Sat 14 Apr 1979	Derby County	A	League	W 2-1
Mon 16 Apr 1979	Leeds United	H	League	D 0-0
Wed 18 Apr 1979	Manchester United	H	League	D 1-1
Sat 21 Apr 1979	Birmingham City	A	League	W 2-0
Wed 25 Apr 1979	FC Köln	A	EC SF 2L	W 1-0
Sat 28 Apr 1979	Liverpool	H	League	D 0-0
Mon 30 Apr 1979	Wolverhampton Wanderers	A	League	L 0-1
Wed 02 May 1979	Southampton	H	League	W 1-0
Sat 05 May 1979	Norwich City	A	League	D 1-1
Wed 09 May 1979	Manchester City	H	League	W 3-1
Tue 15 May 1979	Leeds United	A	League	W 2-1
Fri 18 May 1979	West Bromwich Albion	A	League	W 1-0
Wed 30 May 1979	Malmö	N	EC Final	W 1-0

DIVISION ONE

1	Liverpool	42	30	8	4	85	16	68
2	Nottingham Forest	42	21	18	3	61	26	60
3	West Bromwich Albion	42	24	11	7	72	35	59
4	Everton	42	17	17	8	52	40	51
5	Leeds United	42	18	14	10	70	52	50
6	Ipswich Town	42	20	9	13	63	49	49
7	Arsenal	42	17	14	11	61	48	48
8	Aston Villa	42	15	16	11	59	49	46
9	Manchester United	42	15	15	12	60	63	45
10	Coventry City	42	14	16	12	58	68	44
11	Tottenham Hotspur	42	13	15	14	48	61	41
12	Middlesbrough	42	15	10	17	57	50	40
13	Bristol City	42	15	10	17	47	51	40
14	Southampton	42	12	16	14	47	53	40
15	Manchester City	42	13	13	16	58	56	39
16	Norwich City	42	7	23	12	51	57	37
17	Bolton Wanderers	42	12	11	19	54	75	35
18	Wolverhampton W.	42	13	8	21	44	68	34
19	Derby County	42	10	11	21	44	71	31
20	Queens Park Rangers	42	6	13	23	45	73	25
21	Birmingham City	42	6	10	26	37	64	22
22	Chelsea	42	5	10	27	44	92	20

SQUAD: Viv Anderson, Colin Barrett, Gary Birtles, Ian Bowyer, Steve Burke, Kenny Burns, Frank Clark, Steve Elliott, Ron Fenton, Trevor Francis, Archie Gemmill, Bryn Gunn, Larry Lloyd, John McGovern, Gary Mills, Dave Needham, John O'Hare, Martin O'Neill, John Robertson, Peter Shilton, Steve Sutton, Tony Woodcock, Peter Withe, Chris Woods.

1979/80

Sat 18 Aug 1979	Ipswich Town	A	League	W 1-0
Wed 22 Aug 1979	Stoke City	H	League	W 1-0
Sat 25 Aug 1979	Coventry City	H	League	W 4-1
Wed 29 Aug 1979	Blackburn Rovers	A	LC2 1L	D 1-1
Sat 01 Sep 1979	West Bromwich Albion	A	League	W 5-1
Wed 05 Sep 1979	Blackburn Rovers	H	LC2 2L	W 6-1
Sat 08 Sep 1979	Leeds United	H	League	D 0-0
Sat 15 Sep 1979	Norwich City	A	League	L 1-3
Wed 19 Sep 1979	Öster	H	EC 1R 1L	W 2-0
Sat 22 Sep 1979	Bristol City	A	League	D 1-1
Tues 25 Sep 1979	Middlesbrough	A	LC 3	W 3-1
Sat 29 Sep 1979	Liverpool	H	League	W 1-0
Wed 03 Oct 1979	Öster	A	EC 1R 2L	D 1-1
Sat 06 Oct 1979	Wolverhampton Wanderers	H	League	W 3-2
Wed 10 Oct 1979	Stoke City	A	League	D 1-1
Sat 13 Oct 1979	Manchester City	A	League	L 0-1
Sat 20 Oct 1979	Bolton Wanderers	H	League	W 5-2
Wed 24 oct 1979	Arges Pitesti	H	EC 2R 1L	W 2-0
Sat 27 Oct 1979	Tottenham Hotspur	A	League	L 0-1
Tues 30 Oct 1979	Bristol City	A	LC 4	D 1-1
Sat 03 Nov 1979	Ipswich Town	H	League	W 2-0
Wed 07 Nov 1979	Arges Pitesti	A	EC 2R 2L	W 2-1
Sat 10 Nov 1979	Southampton	A	League	L 1-4
Wed 14 Nov 1979	Bristol City	H	LC 4R	W 3-0
Sat 17 Nov 1979	Brighton & Hove Albion	H	League	L 0-1
Sat 24 Nov 1979	Derby County	A	League	L 1-4
Sat 01 Dec 1979	Arsenal	H	League	D 1-1
Tues 04 Dec 1979	West Ham United	A	LC 5	D 0-0
Sat 08 Dec 1979	Crystal Palace	A	League	L 0-1
Wed 12 Dec 1979	West Ham United	H	LC 5R	W 3-0
Sat 22 Dec 1979	Manchester United	A	League	L 0-3
Wed 26 Dec 1979	Aston Villa	H	League	W 2-1
Sat 29 Dec 1979	Coventry City	A	League	W 3-0
Tue 01 Jan 1980	Everton	A	League	L 0-1
Sat 05 Jan 1980	Leeds United	A	FAC 3	W 4-1
Sat 12 Jan 1980	West Bromwich Albion	H	League	W 3-1
Sat 19 Jan 1980	Leeds United	A	League	W 2-1
Tues 22 Jan 1980	Liverpool	H	LC SF 1L	W 1-0
Sat 26 Jan 1980	Liverpool	A	FAC 4	L 0-2
Wed 30 Jan 1980	FC Barcelona	H	ESC 1L	W 1-0
Wed 05 Feb 1980	FC Barcelona	A	ESC 2L	D 1-1
Sat 09 Feb 1980	Bristol City	H	League	D 0-0
Wed 12 Feb 1980	Liverpool	A	LC SF 2L	D 1-1
Sat 16 Feb 1980	Middlesbrough	H	League	D 2-2
Tue 19 Feb 1980	Liverpool	A	League	L 0-2
Sat 23 Feb 1980	Manchester City	H	League	W 4-0
Sat 01 Mar 1980	Bolton Wanderers	A	League	L 0-1

Wed 05 Mar 1980	Dinamo Berlin	H	EC QF 1L	L 0-1
Tue 11 Mar 1980	Tottenham Hotspur	H	League	W 4-0
Sat 15 Mar 1980	Wolverhampton Wanderers	N	LC Final	L 0-1
Wed 19 Mar 1980	Dinamo Berlin	A	EC QF 2L	W 3-1
Sat 22 Mar 1980	Southampton	H	League	W 2-0
Sat 29 Mar 1980	Brighton & Hove Albion	A	League	L 0-1
Wed 02 Apr 1980	Manchester United	H	League	W 2-0
Sat 05 Apr 1980	Aston Villa	A	League	L 2-3
Wed 09 Apr 1980	Ajax	H	EC SF 1L	W 2-0
Sat 19 Apr 1980	Derby County	H	League	W 1-0
Wed 23 Apr 1980	Ajax	A	EC SF 2L	L 0-1
Sat 26 Apr 1980	Middlesbrough	A	League	D 0-0
Wed 30 Apr 1980	Norwich City	H	League	W 2-0
Sat 03 May 1980	Crystal Palace	H	League	W 4-0
Mon 05 May 1980	Arsenal	A	League	D 0-0
Fri 09 May 1980	Everton	H	League	W 1-0
Mon 12 May 1980	Wolverhampton Wanderers	A	League	L 1-3
Wed 28 May 1980	Hamburg	N	EC Final	W 1-0

DIVISION ONE

1	Liverpool	42	25	10	7	81	30	60
2	Manchester United	42	24	10	8	65	35	58
3	Ipswich Town	42	22	9	11	68	39	53
4	Arsenal	42	18	16	8	52	36	52
5	Nottingham Forest	42	20	8	14	63	43	48
6	Wolverhampton W.	42	19	9	14	58	47	47
7	Aston Villa	42	16	14	12	51	50	46
8	Southampton	42	18	9	15	65	53	45
9	Middlesbrough	42	16	12	14	50	44	44
10	West Bromwich Albion	42	11	19	12	54	50	41
11	Leeds United	42	13	14	15	46	50	40
12	Norwich City	42	13	14	15	58	66	40
13	Crystal Palace	42	12	16	14	41	50	40
14	Tottenham Hotspur	42	15	10	17	52	62	40
15	Coventry City	42	16	7	19	56	66	39
16	Brighton & Hove Albion	42	11	15	16	47	57	37
17	Manchester City	42	12	13	17	43	66	37
18	Stoke City	42	13	10	19	44	58	36
19	Everton	42	9	17	16	43	51	35
20	Bristol City	42	9	13	20	37	66	31
21	Derby County	42	11	8	23	47	67	30
22	Bolton Wanderers	42	5	15	22	38	73	25

SQUAD: Viv Anderson, Gary Birtles, Stan Bowles, Ian Bowyer, Kenny Burns, Ron Fenton, Trevor Francis, Charlie George, Frank Gray, Bryn Gunn, Ada Hartford, Larry Lloyd, John McGovern, Gary Mills, Dave Needham, John O'Hare, Martin O'Neill, John Robertson, Peter Shilton, Steve Sutton, Colin Walsh, Tony Woodcock

1980/81

Sat 16 Aug 1980	Tottenham Hotspur	A	League	L 0-2
Wed 20 Aug 1980	Birmingham City	H	League	W 2-1
Sat 23 Aug 1980	Everton	A	League	D 0-0
Wed 27 Aug 1980	Peterborough United	H	LC2 1L	W 3-0
Sat 30 Aug 1980	Stoke City	H	League	W 5-0
Wed 03 Sep 1980	Peterborough United	A	LC2 2L	D 1-1
Sat 06 Sep 1980	Middlesbrough	A	League	D 0-0
Sat 13 Sep 1980	Manchester City	H	League	W 3-2
Wed 17 Sep 1980	Cska Sofia	A	EC 1R 1L	L 0-1
Sat 20 Sep 1980	Leicester City	H	League	W 5-0
Wed 23 Sep 1980	Bury	A	LC 3	W 7-0
Sat 27 Sep 1980	Arsenal	A	League	L 0-1
Wed 01 Oct 1980	Cska Sofia	H	EC 1R 2L	L 0-1
Sat 04 Oct 1980	Manchester United	H	League	L 1-2
Wed 08 Oct 1980	Sunderland	A	League	D 2-2
Sat 11 Oct 1980	Brighton & Hove Albion	A	League	W 1-0
Sat 18 Oct 1980	West Bromwich Albion	H	League	W 2-1
Wed 22 Oct 1980	Leeds United	H	League	W 2-1
Sat 25 Oct 1980	Norwich City	A	League	D 1-1
Tues 28 Oct 1980	Watford	A	LC 4	L 1-4
Sat 01 Nov 1980	Southampton	H	League	W 2-1
Sat 08 Nov 1980	Liverpool	A	League	D 0-0
Tue 11 Nov 1980	Birmingham City	A	League	L 0-2
Sat 15 Nov 1980	Tottenham Hotspur	H	League	L 0-3
Sat 22 Nov 1980	Ipswich Town	H	League	L 1-2
Wed 25 Nov 1980	Valencia	H	ESC 1L	W 2-1
Sat 29 Nov 1980	Coventry City	A	League	D 1-1
Sat 06 Dec 1980	Crystal Palace	H	League	W 3-0
Sat 13 Dec 1980	Leeds United	A	League	L 0-1
Wed 17 Dec 1980	Valencia	A	ESC 2L	L 0-1
Sat 20 Dec 1980	Sunderland	H	League	W 3-1
Fri 26 Dec 1980	Wolverhampton Wanderers	A	League	W 4-1
Sat 27 Dec 1980	Aston Villa	H	League	D 2-2
Sat 03 Jan 1981	Bolton Wanderers	H	FAC 3	D 3-3
Tues 06 Jan 1981	Bolton Wanderers	A	FAC 3 R	W 1-0
Sat 10 Jan 1981	Ipswich Town	A	League	L 0-2
Sat 24 Jan 1981	Manchester United	H	FAC 4	W 1-0
Sat 31 Jan 1981	Everton	H	League	W 1-0
Sat 07 Feb 1981	Manchester City	A	League	D 1-1
Wed 11 Feb 1981	Nacional	N	WCC	L 0-1
Sat 14 Feb 1981	Bristol City	H	FAC 5	W 2-1
Wed 18 Feb 1981	Stoke City	A	League	W 2-1
Sat 21 Feb 1981	Arsenal	H	League	W 3-1

Sat 28 Feb 1981	Leicester City	A	League	D 1-1
Tue 03 Mar 1981	Middlesbrough	H	League	W 1-0
Sat 07 Mar 1981	Ipswich Town	H	FAC 6	D 3-3
Tues 10 Mar 1981	Ipswich Town	A	FAC 6 R	L 0-1
Sat 14 Mar 1981	Brighton & Hove Albion	H	League	W 4-1
Wed 18 Mar 1981	Manchester United	A	League	D 1-1
Sat 21 Mar 1981	West Bromwich Albion	A	League	L 1-2
Sat 28 Mar 1981	Norwich City	H	League	W 2-1
Sat 04 Apr 1981	Southampton	A	League	L 0-2
Sat 11 Apr 1981	Liverpool	H	League	D 0-0
Sat 18 Apr 1981	Aston Villa	A	League	L 0-2
Mon 20 Apr 1981	Wolverhampton Wanderers	H	League	W 1-0
Sat 25 Apr 1981	Crystal Palace	A	League	W 3-1
Sat 02 May 1981	Coventry City	H	League	D 1-1

DIVISION ONE

1	Aston Villa	42	26	8	8	72	40	60
2	Ipswich Town	42	23	10	9	77	43	56
3	Arsenal	42	19	15	8	61	45	53
4	West Bromwich Albion	42	20	12	10	60	42	52
5	Liverpool	42	17	17	8	62	42	51
6	Southampton	42	20	10	12	76	56	50
7	Nottingham Forest	42	19	12	11	62	44	50
8	Manchester United	42	15	18	9	51	36	48
9	Leeds United	42	17	10	15	39	47	44
10	Tottenham Hotspur	42	14	15	13	70	68	43
11	Stoke City	42	12	18	12	51	60	42
12	Manchester City	42	14	11	17	56	59	39
13	Birmingham City	42	13	12	17	50	61	38
14	Middlesbrough	42	16	5	21	53	61	37
15	Everton	42	13	10	19	55	58	36
16	Coventry City	42	13	10	19	48	68	36
17	Sunderland	42	14	7	21	52	53	35
18	Wolverhampton W.	42	13	9	20	43	55	35
19	Brighton & Hove Albion	42	14	7	21	54	67	35
20	Norwich City	42	13	7	22	49	73	33
21	Leicester City	42	13	6	23	40	67	32
22	Crystal Palace	42	6	7	29	47	83	19

SQUAD: Einar Aas, Viv Anderson, Gary Birtles, Ian Bowyer, Kenny Burns, Ron Fenton, Trevor Francis, Stuart Gray, Frank Gray, Bryn Gunn, Larry Lloyd, John McGovern, Gary Mills, Dave Needham, Martin O'Neill, Raimondo Ponte, John Robertson, Peter Shilton, Lee Smelt, Steve Sutton, Ian Wallace, Colin Walsh, Peter Ward

1981/82

Sat 29 Aug 1981	Southampton	H	League	W 2-1
Mon 31 Aug 1981	Manchester United	A	League	D 0-0
Sat 05 Sep 1981	Birmingham City	A	League	L 3-4
Sat 12 Sep 1981	West Bromwich Albion	H	League	D 0-0
Sat 19 Sep 1981	Stoke City	A	League	W 2-1
Wed 23 Sep 1981	Sunderland	H	League	W 2-0
Sat 26 Sep 1981	Brighton & Hove Albion	H	League	W 2-1
Sat 03 Oct 1981	Tottenham Hotspur	A	League	L 0-3
Tues 06 Oct 1981	Birmingham City	A	LC2 1L	W 3-2
Sat 10 Oct 1981	Middlesbrough	A	League	D 1-1
Sat 17 Oct 1981	Coventry City	H	League	W 2-1
Sat 24 Oct 1981	Manchester City	A	League	D 0-0
Sat 28 Oct 1981	Birmingham City	H	LC2 2L	W 2-1
Sat 31 Oct 1981	Leeds United	H	League	W 2-1
Sat 07 Nov 1981	West Ham United	H	League	D 0-0
Wed 11 Nov 1981	Blackburn Rovers	A	LC 3	W 1-0
Sat 21 Nov 1981	Arsenal	H	League	L 1-2
Wed 25 Nov 1981	Sunderland	A	League	W 3-2
Sat 28 Nov 1981	Aston Villa	A	League	L 1-3
Wed 02 Dec 1981	Tranmere Rovers	H	LC 4	W 2-0
Sat 05 Dec 1981	Liverpool	H	League	L 0-2
Sat 12 Dec 1981	Swansea City	A	League	W 2-1
Sat 02 Jan 1981	Wrexham	H	FAC 3	L 1-3
Sat 09 Jan 1982	Birmingham City	H	League	W 2-1
Tues 18 Jan 1982	Tottenham Hotspur	A	LC 5	L 0-1
Sat 23 Jan 1982	Notts. County	H	League	L 0-2
Sat 30 Jan 1982	Stoke City	H	League	D 0-0
Sat 06 Feb 1982	West Bromwich Albion	A	League	L 1-2
Sat 13 Feb 1982	Southampton	A	League	L 0-2
Tue 16 Feb 1982	Wolverhampton Wanderers	A	League	D 0-0
Sat 20 Feb 1982	Brighton & Hove Albion	A	League	W 1-0
Sat 27 Feb 1982	Middlesbrough	H	League	D 1-1
Tue 09 Mar 1982	Coventry City	A	League	W 1-0
Sat 13 Mar 1982	Manchester City	H	League	D 1-1
Wed 17 Mar 1982	Ipswich Town	H	League	D 1-1
Sat 20 Mar 1982	Leeds United	A	League	D 1-1
Sat 27 Mar 1982	West Ham United	A	League	W 1-0
Sat 03 Apr 1982	Everton	H	League	L 0-1
Sat 10 Apr 1982	Wolverhampton Wanderers	H	League	L 0-1
Mon 12 Apr 1982	Notts. County	A	League	W 2-1
Sat 17 Apr 1982	Arsenal	A	League	L 0-2

Tue 20 Apr 1982	Everton	A	League	L 1-2
Sat 24 Apr 1982	Aston Villa	H	League	D 1-1
Sat 01 May 1982	Liverpool	A	League	L 0-2
Wed 05 May 1982	Manchester United	H	League	L 0-1
Sat 08 May 1982	Swansea City	H	League	L 0-2
Wed 12 May 1982	Tottenham Hotspur	H	League	W 2-0
Sat 15 May 1982	Ipswich Town	A	League	W 3-1

DIVISION ONE

1	Liverpool	42	26	9	7	80	32	87
2	Ipswich Town	42	26	5	11	75	53	83
3	Manchester United	42	22	12	8	59	29	78
4	Tottenham Hotspur	42	20	11	11	67	48	71
5	Arsenal	42	20	11	11	48	37	71
6	Swansea City	42	21	6	15	58	51	69
7	Southampton	42	19	9	14	72	67	66
8	Everton	42	17	13	12	56	50	64
9	West Ham United	42	14	16	12	66	57	58
10	Manchester City	42	15	13	14	49	50	58
11	Aston Villa	42	15	12	15	55	53	57
12	Nottingham Forest	42	15	12	15	42	48	57
13	Brighton & Hove Albion	42	13	13	16	43	52	52
14	Coventry City	42	13	11	18	56	62	50
15	Notts County	42	13	8	21	61	69	47
16	Birmingham City	42	10	14	18	53	61	44
17	West Bromwich Albion	42	11	11	20	46	57	44
18	Stoke City	42	12	8	22	44	63	44
19	Sunderland	42	11	11	20	38	58	44
20	Leeds United	42	10	12	20	39	61	42
21	Wolverhampton W.	42	10	10	22	32	63	40
22	Middlesbrough	42	8	15	19	34	52	39

SQUAD: Einar Aas, Viv Anderson, Ian Bowyer, Kenny Burns, Peter Davenport, Chris Fairclough, Justin Fashanu, Ron Fenton, Trevor Francis, Stuart Gray, Bryn Gunn, Steve Hodge, Steve Kendal, John McGovern, Gary Mills, Dave Needham, Calvin Plummer, Mark Proctor, Neil Redfearn, Juergen Rober, John Robertson, Peter Shilton, Steve Sutton, Ian Wallace, Colin Walsh, Peter Ward, Willie Young,

1982/83

Sat 28 Aug 1982	West Ham United	A	League	W 2-1
Wed 01 Sep 1982	Manchester United	H	League	L 0-3
Sat 04 Sep 1982	Brighton & Hove Albion	H	League	W 4-0
Tue 07 Sep 1982	Liverpool	A	League	L 3-4
Sat 11 Sep 1982	Aston Villa	A	League	L 1-4
Sat 18 Sep 1982	Watford	H	League	W 2-0
Sat 25 Sep 1982	Tottenham Hotspur	A	League	L 1-4
Sat 02 Oct 1982	Stoke City	H	League	W 1-0
Wed 06 Oct 1982	Wba	H	LC 2 1L	W 6-1
Sat 09 Oct 1982	West Bromwich Albion	A	League	L 1-2
Sat 16 Oct 1982	Birmingham City	H	League	D 1-1
Sat 23 Oct 1982	Arsenal	H	League	W 3-0
Tues 26 Oct 1982	Wba	A	LC 2 2L	L 1-3
Sat 30 Oct 1982	Luton Town	A	League	W 2-0
Sat 06 Nov 1982	Ipswich Town	H	League	W 2-1
Sat 10 Nov 1982	Watford	H	LC 3	W 7-3
Sat 13 Nov 1982	Southampton	A	League	D 1-1
Sat 20 Nov 1982	Sunderland	A	League	W 1-0
Sat 27 Nov 1982	Manchester City	H	League	W 3-0
Sat 30 Nov 1982	Brentford	H	LC 4	W 2-0
Sat 04 Dec 1982	Notts. County	A	League	L 2-3
Sat 11 Dec 1982	Swansea City	H	League	W 2-1
Sat 18 Dec 1982	Norwich City	A	League	W 1-0
Mon 27 Dec 1982	Coventry City	H	League	W 4-2
Tue 28 Dec 1982	Everton	A	League	L 1-3
Sat 01 Jan 1983	Sunderland	H	League	D 0-0
Mon 03 Jan 1983	Brighton & Hove Albion	A	League	D 1-1
Sat 08 Jan 1983	Derby County	A	FAC 3	L 0-2
Sat 15 Jan 1983	West Ham United	H	League	W 1-0
Sat 19 Jan 1983	Manchester United	A	LC 5	L 0-4
Sat 22 Jan 1983	Manchester United	A	League	L 0-2
Sat 05 Feb 1983	Aston Villa	H	League	L 1-2
Sat 19 Feb 1983	West Bromwich Albion	H	League	D 0-0
Sat 26 Feb 1983	Birmingham City	A	League	D 1-1
Sat 05 Mar 1983	Arsenal	A	League	D 0-0
Sat 12 Mar 1983	Luton Town	H	League	L 0-1
Wed 16 Mar 1983	Stoke City	A	League	L 0-1
Sat 19 Mar 1983	Ipswich Town	A	League	L 0-2
Sat 26 Mar 1983	Southampton	H	League	L 1-2
Sat 02 Apr 1983	Everton	H	League	W 2-0
Tue 05 Apr 1983	Coventry City	A	League	W 2-1

Sat 09 Apr 1983	Tottenham Hotspur	H	League	D 2-2
Sat 16 Apr 1983	Watford	A	League	W 3-1
Sat 23 Apr 1983	Notts. County	H	League	W 2-1
Sat 30 Apr 1983	Manchester City	A	League	W 2-1
Mon 02 May 1983	Liverpool	H	League	W 1-0
Sat 07 May 1983	Norwich City	H	League	D 2-2
Sat 14 May 1983	Swansea City	A	League	W 3-0

DIVISION ONE

1	Liverpool	42	24	10	8	87	37	82
2	Watford	42	22	5	15	74	57	71
3	Manchester United	42	19	13	10	56	38	70
4	Tottenham Hotspur	42	20	9	13	65	50	69
5	Nottingham Forest	42	20	9	13	62	50	69
6	Aston Villa	42	21	5	16	62	50	68
7	Everton	42	18	10	14	66	48	64
8	West Ham United	42	20	4	18	68	62	64
9	Ipswich Town	42	15	13	14	64	50	58
10	Arsenal	42	16	10	16	58	56	58
11	West Bromwich Albion	42	15	12	15	51	49	57
12	Southampton	42	15	12	15	54	58	57
13	Stoke City	42	16	9	17	53	64	57
14	Norwich City	42	14	12	16	52	58	54
15	Notts County	42	15	7	20	55	71	52
16	Sunderland	42	12	14	16	48	61	50
17	Birmingham City	42	12	14	16	40	55	50
18	Luton Town	42	12	13	17	65	84	49
19	Coventry City	42	13	9	20	48	59	48
20	Manchester City	42	13	8	21	47	70	47
21	Swansea City	42	10	11	21	51	69	41
22	Brighton & Hove Albion	42	9	13	20	38	68	40

SQUAD: Viv Anderson, Gary Birtles, Ian Bowyer, Peter Davenport, Chris Fairclough, Ron Fenton, Stuart Gray, Bryn Gunn, Steve Hodge, Calvin Plummer, Mark Proctor, John Robertson, Peter Shilton, Ron Sinclair, Mark Smalley, Steve Sutton, Kenny Swain, Colin Todd, Ian Wallace, Colin Walsh, Peter Ward, Steve Wigley, Danny Wilson, Willie Young, Hans Van Breukelen, ,

1983/84

Sat 27 Aug 1983	Southampton	H	League	L 0-1
Mon 29 Aug 1983	Manchester United	A	League	W 2-1
Sat 03 Sep 1983	Liverpool	A	League	L 0-1
Wed 07 Sep 1983	Aston Villa	H	League	D 2-2
Sat 10 Sep 1983	Queens Park Rangers	H	League	W 3-2
Werd 14 Sep 1983	Vorwärts Frankfurt	H	UEFA 1R 1L	W 2-0
Sat 17 Sep 1983	Norwich City	A	League	W 3-2
Sat 24 Sep 1983	Luton Town	H	League	W 1-0
Wed 28 Sep 1983	Vorwärts Frankfurt	A	UEFA 1R 2L	W 1-0
Sun 02 Oct 1983	Tottenham Hotspur	A	League	L 1-2
Tues 04 Oct 1983	Wimbledon	A	LC 2 1L	L 0-2
Sun 16 Oct 1983	Notts. County	H	League	W 3-1
Wed 19 Oct 1983	Psv Eindhoven	A	UEFA 2R 1L	W 2-1
Sat 22 Oct 1983	Arsenal	A	League	L 1-4
Wed 26 Oct 183	Wimbledon	H	LC2 2L	D 1-1
Sat 29 Oct 1983	Sunderland	H	League	D 1-1
Wed 2 Nov 1983	Psv Eindhoven	H	UEFA 2R 2L	W 1-0
Sat 05 Nov 1983	Wolverhampton Wanderers	H	League	W 5-0
Sat 12 Nov 1983	Everton	A	League	L 0-1
Sat 19 Nov 1983	Ipswich Town	H	League	W 2-1
Wed 23 Nov 1983	Celtic	H	UEFA 3R 1L	D 0-0
Sat 26 Nov 1983	Stoke City	A	League	D 1-1
Sun 04 Dec 1983	Leicester City	H	League	W 3-2
Wed 07 Dec 1983	Celtic	A	UEFA 3R 2L	W 2-1
Sat 10 Dec 1983	Watford	A	League	L 2-3
Sat 17 Dec 1983	West Ham United	H	League	W 3-0
Mon 26 Dec 1983	Birmingham City	A	League	W 2-1
Wed 28 Dec 1983	Coventry City	H	League	W 3-0
Sat 31 Dec 1983	Liverpool	H	League	L 0-1
Mon 02 Jan 1984	Luton Town	A	League	W 3-2
Sat 07 Jan 1984	Southampton	H	FAC 3	L 1-2
Sat 21 Jan 1984	Norwich City	H	League	W 3-0
Mon 23 Jan 1984	Southampton	A	League	W 1-0
Sat 04 Feb 1984	Tottenham Hotspur	H	League	D 2-2
Wed 08 Feb 1984	West Bromwich Albion	A	League	W 5-0
Sat 11 Feb 1984	Queens Park Rangers	A	League	W 1-0
Sat 18 Feb 1984	Sunderland	A	League	D 1-1
Sat 25 Feb 1984	Arsenal	H	League	L 0-1
Sat 03 Mar 1984	Wolverhampton Wanderers	A	League	L 0-1
Wed 07 Mar 1984	Sturm Graz	H	UEFA QF 1L	W 1-0
Tue 13 Mar 1984	Everton	H	League	W 1-0

Sat 17 Mar 1984	Aston Villa	A	League	L 0-1
Wed 21 Mar 1984	Sturm Graz	A	UEFA QF 2L	D 1-1
Sat 31 Mar 1984	Notts. County	A	League	D 0-0
Sat 07 Apr 1984	West Bromwich Albion	H	League	W 3-1
Wed 11 Apr 1984	Anderlecht	H	UEFA SF 1L	W 2-0
Sat 14 Apr 1984	Ipswich Town	A	League	D 2-2
Tue 17 Apr 1984	Coventry City	A	League	L 1-2
Sat 21 Apr 1984	Birmingham City	H	League	W 5-1
Wed 25 Apr 1984	Anderlecht	A	UEFA SF 2L	L 0-3
Sat 28 Apr 1984	Stoke City	H	League	D 0-0
Sat 05 May 1984	Leicester City	A	League	L 1-2
Mon 07 May 1984	Watford	H	League	W 5-1
Sat 12 May 1984	West Ham United	A	League	W 2-1
Wed 16 May 1984	Manchester United	H	League	W 2-0

DIVISION ONE

1	Liverpool	42	22	14	6	73	32	80
2	Southampton	42	22	11	9	66	38	77
3	Nottingham Forest	42	22	8	12	76	45	74
4	Manchester United	42	20	14	8	71	41	74
5	Queens Park Rangers	42	22	7	13	67	37	73
6	Arsenal	42	18	9	15	74	60	63
7	Everton	42	16	14	12	44	42	62
8	Tottenham Hotspur	42	17	10	15	64	65	61
9	West Ham United	42	17	9	16	60	55	60
10	Aston Villa	42	17	9	16	59	61	60
11	Watford	42	16	9	17	68	77	57
12	Ipswich Town	42	15	8	19	55	57	53
13	Sunderland	42	13	13	16	42	53	52
14	Norwich City	42	12	15	15	48	49	51
15	Leicester City	42	13	12	17	65	68	51
16	Luton Town	42	14	9	19	53	66	51
17	West Bromwich Albion	42	14	9	19	48	62	51
18	Stoke City	42	13	11	18	44	63	50
19	Coventry City	42	13	11	18	57	77	50
20	Birmingham City	42	12	12	18	39	50	48
21	Notts County	42	10	11	21	50	72	41
22	Wolverhampton W.	42	6	11	25	27	80	29

SQUAD: Viv Anderson, Gary Birtles, Ian Bowyer, Thomas Danks, Peter Davenport, Chris Fairclough, Ron Fenton, Bryn Gunn, Paul Hart, Kevin Hitchcock, Steve Hodge, Gary Mills, David Riley, Liam Robertson, Ron Sinclair, Mark Smalley, Steve Sutton, Kenny Swain, Frans Thijssen, Colin Todd, Des Walker, Ian Wallace, Colin Walsh, Steve Wigley, Hans Van Breukelen.

1984/85

Sat 25 Aug 1984	Sheffield Wednesday	A	League	L 1-3
Wed 29 Aug 1984	Arsenal	H	League	W 2-0
Sat 01 Sep 1984	Sunderland	H	League	W 3-1
Wed 05 Sep 1984	Aston Villa	A	League	W 5-0
Sat 08 Sep 1984	Queens Park Rangers	A	League	L 0-3
Sun 16 Sep 1984	Luton Town	H	League	W 3-1
Wed 19 Sep 1984	Club Brugge	H	UEFA 1R 1L	D 0-0
Sat 22 Sep 1984	West Ham United	A	League	D 0-0
Tues 25 Sep 1984	Portsmouth	A	LC 2R 1L	L 0-1
Sat 29 Sep 1984	Norwich City	H	League	W 3-1
Wed 03 Oct 1984	Club Brugge	A	UEFA 1R 2L	L 0-1
Sat 06 Oct 1984	Stoke City	H	League	D 1-1
Wed 10 Oct 1984	Portsmouth	H	LC 2R 2L	W 3-0
Sat 13 Oct 1984	West Bromwich Albion	A	League	L 1-4
Sat 20 Oct 1984	Newcastle United	A	League	D 1-1
Sun 28 Oct 1984	Liverpool	H	League	L 0-2
Wed 31 Oct 1984	Sunderland	H	LC 3	D 1-1
Sat 03 Nov 1984	Southampton	A	League	L 0-1
Tues 06 Nov 1984	Sunderland	A	LC 3 R	L 0-1
Sat 10 Nov 1984	Tottenham Hotspur	H	League	L 1-2
Sat 17 Nov 1984	Coventry City	A	League	W 3-1
Sun 25 Nov 1984	Leicester City	H	League	W 2-1
Sat 01 Dec 1984	Watford	A	League	L 0-2
Sat 08 Dec 1984	Manchester United	H	League	W 3-2
Sat 15 Dec 1984	Everton	A	League	L 0-5
Sun 23 Dec 1984	Sunderland	A	League	W 2-0
Wed 26 Dec 1984	Ipswich Town	H	League	W 2-0
Sat 29 Dec 1984	Aston Villa	H	League	W 3-2
Tue 01 Jan 1985	Chelsea	A	League	L 0-1
Sat 06 Jan 1985	Newcastle United	H	FAC 3	D 1-1
Tues 09 Jan 1985	Newcastle United	A	FAC 3 R	W 3-1
Sat 26 Jan 1985	Wimbledon	H	FAC 4	D 0-0
Sat 30 Jan 1985	Wimbledon	A	FAC 4 R	L 0-1
Sat 02 Feb 1985	Norwich City	A	League	W 1-0
Sat 09 Feb 1985	Queens Park Rangers	H	League	W 2-0
Sat 23 Feb 1985	Southampton	H	League	W 2-0
Sat 02 Mar 1985	Liverpool	A	League	L 0-1
Sat 09 Mar 1985	Newcastle United	H	League	D 0-0
Sat 16 Mar 1985	West Bromwich Albion	H	League	L 1-2
Wed 20 Mar 1985	Sheffield Wednesday	H	League	D 0-0

Sat 23 Mar 1985	Stoke City	A	League	W 4-1
Sat 30 Mar 1985	West Ham United	H	League	L 1-2
Sat 06 Apr 1985	Ipswich Town	A	League	L 0-1
Wed 10 Apr 1985	Chelsea	H	League	W 2-0
Sat 13 Apr 1985	Arsenal	A	League	D 1-1
Sat 20 Apr 1985	Coventry City	H	League	W 2-0
Wed 24 Apr 1985	Luton Town	A	League	W 2-1
Sat 27 Apr 1985	Leicester City	A	League	L 0-1
Sat 04 May 1985	Watford	H	League	D 1-1
Mon 06 May 1985	Manchester United	A	League	L 0-2
Sat 11 May 1985	Everton	H	League	W 1-0
Fri 17 May 1985	Tottenham Hotspur	A	League	L 0-1

DIVISION ONE

1	Everton	42	28	6	8	88	43	90
2	Liverpool	42	22	11	9	68	35	77
3	Tottenham Hotspur	42	23	8	11	78	51	77
4	Manchester United	42	22	10	10	77	47	76
5	Southampton	42	19	11	12	56	47	68
6	Chelsea	42	18	12	12	63	48	66
7	Arsenal	42	19	9	14	61	49	66
8	Sheffield Wednesday	42	17	14	11	58	45	65
9	Nottingham Forest	42	19	7	16	56	48	64
10	Aston Villa	42	15	11	16	60	60	56
11	Watford	42	14	13	15	81	71	55
12	West Bromwich Albion	42	16	7	19	58	62	55
13	Luton Town	42	15	9	18	57	61	54
14	Newcastle United	42	13	13	16	55	70	52
15	Leicester City	42	15	6	21	65	73	51
16	West Ham United	42	13	12	17	51	68	51
17	Ipswich Town	42	13	11	18	46	57	50
18	Coventry City	42	15	5	22	47	64	50
19	Queens Park Rangers	42	13	11	18	53	72	50
20	Norwich City	42	13	10	19	46	64	49
21	Sunderland	42	10	10	22	40	62	40
22	Stoke City	42	3	8	31	24	91	17

SQUAD: Gary Birtles, Ian Bowyer, David Campbell, Franz Carr, Trevor Christie, Nigel Clough, Thomas Danks, Peter Davenport, Alan Davidson, Chris Fairclough, Ron Fenton, Gary Fleming, Bryn Gunn, Paul Hart, Steve Hodge, Jim McInally, Gary Megson, Johnny Metgod, Gary Mills, Stuart Pearce, Paul Raynor, David Riley, Hans Segers, Ron Sinclair, Mark Smalley, Steve Sutton, Kenny Swain, Des Walker, Colin Walsh, Steve Wigley,

1985/86

Sat 17 Aug 1985	Luton Town	A	League	D 1-1
Wed 21 Aug 1985	Sheffield Wednesday	H	League	L 0-1
Sat 24 Aug 1985	Southampton	H	League	W 2-1
Tue 27 Aug 1985	Queens Park Rangers	A	League	L 1-2
Sat 31 Aug 1985	Manchester United	H	League	L 1-3
Tue 03 Sep 1985	Liverpool	A	League	L 0-2
Sun 08 Sep 1985	Leicester City	A	League	W 3-0
Sat 14 Sep 1985	Tottenham Hotspur	H	League	L 0-1
Sat 21 Sep 1985	Watford	H	League	W 3-2
Wed 25 Sep 1985	Bolton Wanderers	H	LC 2R 1L	W 4-0
Sat 28 Sep 1985	West Ham United	A	League	L 2-4
Sat 05 Oct 1985	Ipswich Town	H	League	W 3-1
Tues 08 Oct 1985	Bolton Wanderers	A	LC 2R 2L	W 3-0
Sat 12 Oct 1985	Aston Villa	A	League	W 2-1
Sat 19 Oct 1985	Newcastle United	A	League	W 3-0
Sat 26 Oct 1985	Arsenal	H	League	W 3-2
Wed 30 Oct 1985	Derby County	A	LC 3R	W 2-1
Sun 03 Nov 1985	West Bromwich Albion	H	League	W 2-1
Sat 09 Nov 1985	Chelsea	A	League	L 2-4
Sat 16 Nov 1985	Manchester City	H	League	L 0-2
Sat 23 Nov 1985	Everton	A	League	D 1-1
Mon 25 Nov 1985	Qpr	A	LC4R	L 1-3
Sun 01 Dec 1985	Oxford United	H	League	D 1-1
Sat 07 Dec 1985	Sheffield Wednesday	A	League	L 1-2
Sat 14 Dec 1985	Luton Town	H	League	W 2-0
Fri 20 Dec 1985	Southampton	A	League	L 1-3
Thu 26 Dec 1985	Birmingham City	A	League	W 1-0
Sat 28 Dec 1985	Liverpool	H	League	D 1-1
Wed 01 Jan 1986	Coventry City	H	League	W 5-2
Sat 04 Jan 1986	Blackburn Rovers	H	FAC 3	D 1-1
Sat 11 Jan 1986	Tottenham Hotspur	A	League	W 3-0
Mon 13 Feb 1986	Blackburn Rovers	A	FAC 3 R	L 2-3
Sat 18 Jan 1986	Manchester United	A	League	W 3-2
Sat 01 Feb 1986	Queens Park Rangers	H	League	W 4-0
Sat 08 Feb 1986	Newcastle United	H	League	L 1-2
Sat 08 Mar 1986	Ipswich Town	A	League	L 0-1
Sat 15 Mar 1986	Aston Villa	H	League	D 1-1
Sat 22 Mar 1986	Leicester City	H	League	W 4-3
Sat 29 Mar 1986	Coventry City	A	League	D 0-0
Mon 31 Mar 1986	Birmingham City	H	League	W 3-0

Wed 02 Apr 1986	West Ham United	H	League	W 2-1
Sat 05 Apr 1986	West Bromwich Albion	A	League	D 1-1
Tue 08 Apr 1986	Arsenal	A	League	D 1-1
Sat 12 Apr 1986	Chelsea	H	League	D 0-0
Sat 19 Apr 1986	Manchester City	A	League	W 2-1
Mon 21 Apr 1986	Watford	A	League	D 1-1
Sat 26 Apr 1986	Everton	H	League	D 0-0
Sat 03 May 1986	Oxford United	A	League	W 2-1

DIVISION ONE

1	Liverpool	42	26	10	6	89	37	88
2	Everton	42	26	8	8	87	41	86
3	West Ham United	42	26	6	10	74	40	84
4	Manchester United	42	22	10	10	70	36	76
5	Sheffield Wednesday	42	21	10	11	63	54	73
6	Chelsea	42	20	11	11	57	56	71
7	Arsenal	42	20	9	13	49	47	69
8	Nottingham Forest	42	19	11	12	69	53	68
9	Luton Town	42	18	12	12	61	44	66
10	Tottenham Hotspur	42	19	8	15	74	52	65
11	Newcastle United	42	17	12	13	67	72	63
12	Watford	42	16	11	15	69	62	59
13	Queens Park Rangers	42	15	7	20	53	64	52
14	Southampton	42	12	10	20	51	62	46
15	Manchester City	42	11	12	19	43	57	45
16	Aston Villa	42	10	14	18	51	67	44
17	Coventry City	42	11	10	21	48	71	43
18	Oxford United	42	10	12	20	62	80	42
19	Leicester City	42	10	12	20	54	76	42
20	Ipswich Town	42	11	8	23	32	55	41
21	Birmingham City	42	8	5	29	30	73	29
22	West Bromwich Albion	42	4	12	26	35	89	24

SQUAD: Gary Birtles, Ian Bowyer, Ian Butterworth, David Campbell, Franz Carr, Trevor Christie, Nigel Clough, Paul Crichton, Thomas Danks, Peter Davenport, Chris Fairclough, Ron Fenton, Gary Fleming, Steve Hodge, Jim McInally, Johnny Metgod, Gary Mills, Stuart Pearce, Brian Rice, David Riley, John Robertson, Hans Segers, Ron Sinclair, Steve Sutton, Des Walker, Colin Walsh, Darren Wassall, Neil Webb, Steve Wigley, Brett Williams.

1986/87

Sat 23 Aug 1986	Everton	A	League	L 0-2
Wed 27 Aug 1986	Charlton Athletic	H	League	W 4-0
Sat 30 Aug 1986	Watford	H	League	D 1-1
Tue 02 Sep 1986	West Ham United	A	League	W 2-1
Sat 06 Sep 1986	Southampton	A	League	W 3-1
Sat 13 Sep 1986	Aston Villa	H	League	W 6-0
Sat 20 Sep 1986	Chelsea	A	League	W 6-2
Wed 24 Sep 1986	Brighton & Hove Albion	A	LC 2R 1L	D 0-0
Sat 27 Sep 1986	Arsenal	H	League	W 1-0
Sat 04 Oct 1986	Manchester United	H	League	D 1-1
Wed 08 Oct 1986	Brighton & Hove Albion	H	LC 2R 2L	W 3-0
Sat 11 Oct 1986	Leicester City	A	League	L 1-3
Sat 18 Oct 1986	Queens Park Rangers	H	League	W 1-0
Sat 25 Oct 1986	Oxford United	A	League	L 1-2
Wed 29 Oct 1986	Crystal Palace	A	LC 3	D 2-2
Sat 01 Nov 1986	Sheffield Wednesday	H	League	W 3-2
Wed 05 Nov 1986	Crystal Palace	H	LC 3 R	W 1-0
Sat 08 Nov 1986	Coventry City	A	League	L 0-1
Sat 15 Nov 1986	Luton Town	A	League	L 2-4
Wed 19 Nov 1986	Bradford City	A	LC 4	W 5-0
Sat 22 Nov 1986	Wimbledon	H	League	W 3-2
Sat 29 Nov 1986	Tottenham Hotspur	A	League	W 3-2
Sat 06 Dec 1986	Manchester City	H	League	W 2-0
Sat 13 Dec 1986	Newcastle United	A	League	L 2-3
Sat 20 Dec 1986	Southampton	H	League	D 0-0
Fri 26 Dec 1986	Norwich City	A	League	L 1-2
Sun 28 Dec 1986	Luton Town	H	League	D 2-2
Thu 01 Jan 1987	Liverpool	H	League	D 1-1
Sat 03 Jan 1987	Aston Villa	A	League	D 0-0
Sun 11 Jan 1987	Crystal Palace	A	FAC 3	L 0-1
Wed 21 Jan 1987	Arsenal	A	LC 5	L 0-2
Sun 25 Jan 1987	Everton	H	League	W 1-0
Sat 31 Jan 1987	Charlton Athletic	A	League	W 1-0
Sat 07 Feb 1987	Watford	A	League	D 1-1
Sat 14 Feb 1987	West Ham United	H	League	D 1-1
Sat 28 Feb 1987	Chelsea	H	League	L 0-1
Sat 07 Mar 1987	Oxford United	H	League	W 2-0
Sat 14 Mar 1987	Queens Park Rangers	A	League	L 1-3
Tue 17 Mar 1987	Arsenal	A	League	D 0-0
Sun 22 Mar 1987	Leicester City	H	League	W 2-1

Sat 28 Mar 1987	Manchester United	A	League	L 0-2
Sat 04 Apr 1987	Coventry City	H	League	D 0-0
Tue 14 Apr 1987	Sheffield Wednesday	A	League	W 3-2
Sat 18 Apr 1987	Liverpool	A	League	L 0-3
Mon 20 Apr 1987	Norwich City	H	League	D 1-1
Sat 25 Apr 1987	Wimbledon	A	League	L 1-2
Sat 02 May 1987	Tottenham Hotspur	H	League	W 2-0
Mon 04 May 1987	Manchester City	A	League	L 0-1
Sat 09 May 1987	Newcastle United	H	League	W 2-1

DIVISION ONE

1	Everton	42	26	8	8	76	31	86
2	Liverpool	42	23	8	11	72	42	77
3	Tottenham Hotspur	42	21	8	13	68	43	71
4	Arsenal	42	20	10	12	58	35	70
5	Norwich City	42	17	17	8	53	51	68
6	Wimbledon	42	19	9	14	57	50	66
7	Luton Town	42	18	12	12	47	45	66
8	Nottingham Forest	42	18	11	13	64	51	65
9	Watford	42	18	9	15	67	54	63
10	Coventry City	42	17	12	13	50	45	63
11	Manchester United	42	14	14	14	52	45	56
12	Southampton	42	14	10	18	69	68	52
13	Sheffield Wednesday	42	13	13	16	58	59	52
14	Chelsea	42	13	13	16	53	64	52
15	West Ham United	42	14	10	18	52	67	52
16	Queens Park Rangers	42	13	11	18	48	64	50
17	Newcastle United	42	12	11	19	47	65	47
18	Oxford United	42	11	13	18	44	69	46
19	Charlton Athletic	42	11	11	20	45	55	44
20	Leicester City	42	11	9	22	54	76	42
21	Manchester City	42	8	15	19	36	57	39
22	Aston Villa	42	8	12	22	45	79	36

SQUAD: Gary Birtles, Ian Bowyer, Ian Butterworth, David Campbell, Franz Carr, Steve Chettle, Nigel Clough, Paul Crichton, Chris Fairclough, Ron Fenton, Gary Fleming, Colin Foster, Lee Glover, Johnny Metgod, Gary Mills, Kjetll Osvold, Stuart Pearce, Brian Rice, David Riley, Hans Segers, Phil Starbuck, Steve Sutton, Des Walker, Colin Walsh, Darren Wassall, Neil Webb, Paul Wilkinson, Brett Williams.

1987/88

Sat 15 Aug 1987	Charlton Athletic	A	League	W 2-1
Wed 19 Aug 1987	Watford	H	League	W 1-0
Sat 22 Aug 1987	Everton	H	League	D 0-0
Sat 29 Aug 1987	Newcastle United	A	League	W 1-0
Wed 02 Sep 1987	Southampton	H	League	D 3-3
Sat 05 Sep 1987	Chelsea	A	League	L 3-4
Sat 12 Sep 1987	Arsenal	H	League	L 0-1
Sat 19 Sep 1987	Coventry City	A	League	W 3-0
Wed 23 Sep 1987	Hereford United	H	LC 2R 1L	W 5-0
Sat 26 Sep 1987	Norwich City	A	League	W 2-0
Wed 07 Oct 1987	Hereford United	A	LC 2R 2L	D 1-1
Sat 10 Oct 1987	Derby County	A	League	W 1-0
Sat 17 Oct 1987	Sheffield Wednesday	H	League	W 3-0
Sat 24 Oct 1987	Tottenham Hotspur	H	League	W 3-0
Tue 27 Oct 1987	Manchester City	A	LC 3	L 0-3
Sat 31 Oct 1987	Manchester United	A	League	D 2-2
Sat 14 Nov 1987	Portsmouth	H	League	W 5-0
Sat 21 Nov 1987	West Ham United	A	League	L 2-3
Sat 05 Dec 1987	Wimbledon	A	League	D 1-1
Sun 13 Dec 1987	Queens Park Rangers	H	League	W 4-0
Sat 19 Dec 1987	Oxford United	A	League	W 2-0
Sat 26 Dec 1987	Arsenal	A	League	W 2-0
Mon 28 Dec 1987	Coventry City	H	League	W 4-1
Fri 01 Jan 1988	Newcastle United	H	League	L 0-2
Sun 03 Jan 1988	Everton	A	League	L 0-1
Sat 09 Jan 1988	Halifax Town	A	FAC 3	W 4-0
Sat 16 Jan 1988	Charlton Athletic	H	League	D 2-2
Sat 23 Jan 1988	Watford	A	League	D 0-0
Sat 30 Jan 1988	Leyton Orient	A	FAC 4	W 2-1
Sat 06 Feb 1988	Chelsea	H	League	W 3-2
Sat 13 Feb 1988	Southampton	A	League	D 1-1
Sat 20 Feb 1988	Birmingham City	A	FAC 5	W 1-0
Sat 05 Mar 1988	Sheffield Wednesday	A	League	W 1-0
Sat 12 Mar 1988	Arsenal	A	FAC 6	W 2-1
Wed 16 Mar 1988	Queens Park Rangers	A	League	L 1-2
Sat 19 Mar 1988	Manchester United	H	League	D 0-0
Sat 26 Mar 1988	Tottenham Hotspur	A	League	D 1-1
Wed 30 Mar 1988	Derby County	H	League	W 2-1
Sat 02 Apr 1988	Liverpool	H	League	W 2-1
Mon 04 Apr 1988	Portsmouth	A	League	W 1-0
Sat 09 Apr 1988	Liverpool	N	FAC SF	L 1-2

Wed 13 Apr 1988	Liverpool	A	League	L 0-5
Wed 20 Apr 1988	West Ham United	H	League	D 0-0
Sat 30 Apr 1988	Wimbledon	H	League	D 0-0
Wed 04 May 1988	Norwich City	H	League	W 2-0
Sat 07 May 1988	Oxford United	H	League	W 5-3
Fri 13 May 1988	Luton Town	A	League	D 1-1
Sun 15 May 1988	Luton Town	H	League	D 1-1

DIVISION ONE

1	Liverpool	40	26	12	2	87	24	90
2	Manchester United	40	23	12	5	71	38	81
3	Nottingham Forest	40	20	13	7	67	39	73
4	Everton	40	19	13	8	53	27	70
5	Queens Park Rangers	40	19	10	11	48	38	67
6	Arsenal	40	18	12	10	58	39	66
7	Wimbledon	40	14	15	11	58	47	57
8	Newcastle United	40	14	14	12	55	53	56
9	Luton Town	40	14	11	15	57	58	53
10	Coventry City	40	13	14	13	46	53	53
11	Sheffield Wednesday	40	15	8	17	52	66	53
12	Southampton	40	12	14	14	49	53	50
13	Tottenham Hotspur	40	12	11	17	38	48	47
14	Norwich City	40	12	9	19	40	52	45
15	Derby County	40	10	13	17	35	45	43
16	West Ham United	40	9	15	16	40	52	42
17	Charlton Athletic	40	9	15	16	38	52	42
18	Chelsea	40	9	15	16	50	68	42
19	Portsmouth	40	7	14	19	36	66	35
20	Watford	40	7	11	22	27	51	32
21	Oxford United	40	6	13	21	44	80	31

SQUAD: David Campbell, Franz Carr, Gary Charles, Steve Chettle, Nigel Clough, Paul Crichton, Gary Crosby, Mark Crossley, Gary Fleming, Colin Foster, Tommy Gaynor, Lee Glover, Johnny Metgod, Gary Mills, Kjetll Osvold, Garry Parker, Stuart Pearce, Calvin Plummer, Brian Rice, Martin Scott, Hans Segers, Phil Starbuck, Steve Sutton, Des Walker, Darren Wassall, Neil Webb, Paul Wilkinson, Brett Williams, Terry Wilson, ,

1988/89

Sat 27 Aug 1988	Norwich City	A	League	L 1-2
Sat 03 Sep 1988	Sheffield Wednesday	H	League	D 1-1
Sat 10 Sep 1988	Everton	A	League	D 1-1
Sat 17 Sep 1988	Derby County	H	League	D 1-1
Sat 24 Sep 1988	Aston Villa	A	League	D 1-1
Wed 28 Sep 1988	Chester City	H	LC 2R 1L	W 6-0
Sat 01 Oct 1988	Luton Town	H	League	D 0-0
Sat 08 Oct 1988	Queens Park Rangers	A	League	W 2-1
Wed 12 Oct 1988	Chester City	A	LC 2R 2L	W 4-0
Sat 22 Oct 1988	Millwall	A	League	D 2-2
Wed 26 Oct 1988	Liverpool	H	League	W 2-1
Sat 29 Oct 1988	Newcastle United	A	League	W 1-0
Wed 02 Nov 1988	Coventry City	H	LC 3	W 3-2
Sun 06 Nov 1988	Arsenal	H	League	L 1-4
Sat 12 Nov 1988	West Ham United	A	League	D 3-3
Sat 19 Nov 1988	Coventry City	H	League	D 0-0
Sat 26 Nov 1988	Charlton Athletic	A	League	W 1-0
Wed 30 Nov 1988	Leicester City	A	LC 4	D 0-0
Sat 03 Dec 1988	Middlesbrough	H	League	D 2-2
Sat 10 Dec 1988	Southampton	A	League	D 1-1
Wed 14 Dec 1988	Leicester City	H	LC 4 R	W 2-1
Sun 18 Dec 1988	Wimbledon	H	League	L 0-1
Mon 26 Dec 1988	Manchester United	A	League	L 0-2
Sat 31 Dec 1988	Sheffield Wednesday	A	League	W 3-0
Mon 02 Jan 1989	Everton	H	League	W 2-0
Sat 07 Jan 1989	Ipswich Town	H	FAC 3	W 3-0
Sun 15 Jan 1989	Tottenham Hotspur	A	League	W 2-1
Wed 18 Jan 1989	Queens Park Rangers	H	LC 5	W 5-2
Sat 21 Jan 1989	Aston Villa	H	League	W 4-0
Sat 28 Jan 1989	Leeds United	H	FAC 4	W 2-0
Sat 04 Feb 1989	Luton Town	A	League	W 3-2
Sat 11 Feb 1989	Queens Park Rangers	H	League	D 0-0
Wed 15 Feb 1989	Bristol City	H	LC SF 1L	D 1-1
Sun 19 Feb 1989	Watford	A	F.A. Cup	W 3-0
Sun 26 Feb 1989	Bristol City	A	LC SF 2L	W 1-0
Sat 11 Mar 1989	Arsenal	A	League	W 3-1
Wed 15 Mar 1989	Newcastle United	H	League	D 1-1
Sat 18 Mar 1989	Manchester United	A	FAC 6	W 1-0
Wed 22 Mar 1989	Tottenham Hotspur	H	League	L 1-2
Sat 25 Mar 1989	Derby County	A	League	W 2-0
Mon 27 Mar 1989	Manchester United	H	League	W 2-0
Sat 01 Apr 1989	Wimbledon	A	League	L 1-4

Wed 05 Apr 1989	Norwich City	H	League	W 2-0
Sun 09 Apr 1989	Luton Town	N	LC Final	W 3-1
Wed 12 Apr 1989	Southampton	H	League	W 3-0
Sat 22 Apr 1989	Middlesbrough	A	League	W 4-3
Wed 03 May 1989	Millwall	H	League	W 4-1
Sun 07 May 1989	Liverpool	N	FAC SF	L 1-3
Wed 10 May 1989	Liverpool	A	League	L 0-1
Sat 13 May 1989	Charlton Athletic	H	League	W 4-0
Mon 15 May 1989	Coventry City	A	League	D 2-2
Thu 18 May 1989	West Ham United	H	League	L 1-2

DIVISION ONE

1	Arsenal	38	22	10	6	73	36	76
2	Liverpool	38	22	10	6	65	28	76
3	Nottingham Forest	38	17	13	8	64	43	64
4	Norwich City	38	17	11	10	48	45	62
5	Derby County	38	17	7	14	40	38	58
6	Tottenham Hotspur	38	15	12	11	60	46	57
7	Coventry City	38	14	13	11	47	42	55
8	Everton	38	14	12	12	50	45	54
9	Queens Park Rangers	38	14	11	13	43	37	53
10	Millwall	38	14	11	13	47	52	53
11	Manchester United	38	13	12	13	45	35	51
12	Wimbledon	38	14	9	15	50	46	51
13	Southampton	38	10	15	13	52	66	45
14	Charlton Athletic	38	10	12	16	44	58	42
15	Sheffield Wednesday	38	10	12	16	34	51	42
16	Luton Town	38	10	11	17	42	52	41
17	Aston Villa	38	9	13	16	45	56	40
18	Middlesbrough	38	9	12	17	44	61	39
19	West Ham United	38	10	8	20	37	62	38
20	Newcastle United	38	7	10	21	32	63	31

SQUAD: Franz Carr, Lee Chapman, Gary Charles, Steve Chettle, Nigel Clough, Paul Crichton, Gary Crosby, Mark Crossley, Sean Dyche, Gary Fleming, Colin Foster, Tommy Gaynor, Lee Glover, Steve Hodge, Brian Laws, Andy Marriott, Garry Parker, Stuart Pearce, Brian Rice, Hans Segers, Phil Starbuck, Steve Sutton, Justin Walker, Des Walker, Darren Wassall, Neil Webb, Paul Wilkinson, Brett Williams, Terry Wilson,

1989/90

Date	Opponent	H/A	Competition	Result
Sat 19 Aug 1989	ASTON VILLA	H	League	D 1-1
Wed 23 Aug 1989	Norwich City	A	League	D 1-1
Sat 26 Aug 1989	Millwall	A	League	L 0-1
Wed 30 Aug 1989	DERBY COUNTY	H	League	W 2-1
Sat 09 Sep 1989	Chelsea	A	League	D 2-2
Sat 16 Sep 1989	ARSENAL	H	League	L 1-2
Wed 20 Sep 1989	HUDDERSFIELD TOWN	H	LC 2R 1L	D 1-1
Sat 23 Sep 1989	Crystal Palace	A	League	L 0-1
Sat 30 Sep 1989	CHARLTON ATHLETIC	H	League	W 2-0
Tue 03 Oct 1989	Huddersfield Town	A	LC 2R 2L	D 3-3
Sat 14 Oct 1989	Coventry City	A	League	W 2-0
Sat 21 Oct 1989	Wimbledon	A	League	W 3-1
Tue 24 Oct 1989	Crystal Palace	A	LC 3	D 0-0
Sat 28 Oct 1989	QUEENS PARK RANGERS	H	League	D 2-2
Wed 01 Nov 1989	CRYSTAL PALACE	H	LC 3 R	W 5-0
Sat 04 Nov 1989	SHEFFIELD WEDNESDAY	H	League	L 0-1
Sun 12 Nov 1989	Manchester United	A	League	L 0-1
Sat 18 Nov 1989	Manchester City	A	League	W 3-0
Wed 22 Nov 1989	EVERTON	H	LC 4	W 1-0
Sat 25 Nov 1989	EVERTON	H	League	W 1-0
Sat 02 Dec 1989	Aston Villa	A	League	L 1-2
Sat 09 Dec 1989	NORWICH CITY	H	League	L 0-1
Sun 17 Dec 1989	SOUTHAMPTON	H	League	W 2-0
Tue 26 Dec 1989	Luton Town	A	League	D 1-1
Sat 30 Dec 1989	Tottenham Hotspur	A	League	W 3-2
Mon 01 Jan 1990	LIVERPOOL	H	League	D 2-2
Sun 07 Jan 1990	MANCHESTER UNITED	H	FAC 3	L 0-1
Sat 13 Jan 1990	MILLWALL	H	League	W 3-1
Wed 17 Jan 1990	TOTTENHAM HOTSPUR	H	LC 5	D 2-2
Sat 20 Jan 1990	Derby County	A	League	W 2-0
Wed 24 Jan 1990	Tottenham Hotspur	A	LC 5 R	W 3-2
Sat 03 Feb 1990	CRYSTAL PALACE	H	League	W 3-1
Sun 11 Feb 1990	COVENTRY CITY	H	LC SF 1L	W 2-1
Sat 17 Feb 1990	CHELSEA	H	League	D 1-1
Sun 25 Feb 1990	Coventry City	A	LC SF 2L	D 0-0
Sat 03 Mar 1990	MANCHESTER CITY	H	League	W 1-0
Wed 07 Mar 1990	Arsenal	A	League	L 0-3
Sat 10 Mar 1990	COVENTRY CITY	H	League	L 2-4
Sat 17 Mar 1990	Charlton Athletic	A	League	D 1-1

Sat 24 Mar 1990	Queens Park Rangers	A	League	L 0-2
Sat 31 Mar 1990	WIMBLEDON	H	League	L 0-1
Wed 04 Apr 1990	Everton	A	League	L 0-4
Sat 07 Apr 1990	TOTTENHAM HOTSPUR	H	League	L 1-3
Sat 14 Apr 1990	Liverpool	A	League	D 2-2
Mon 16 Apr 1990	LUTON TOWN	H	League	W 3-0
Sat 21 Apr 1990	Southampton	A	League	L 0-2
Sun 29 Apr 1990	Oldham Athletic	N	LC Final	W 1-0
Wed 02 May 1990	MANCHESTER UNITED	H	League	W 4-0
Sat 05 May 1990	Sheffield Wednesday	A	League	W 3-0

DIVISION ONE

1	Liverpool	38	23	10	5	78	37	79
2	Aston Villa	38	21	7	10	57	38	70
3	Tottenham Hotspur	38	19	6	13	59	47	63
4	Arsenal	38	18	8	12	54	38	62
5	Chelsea	38	16	12	10	58	50	60
6	Everton	38	17	8	13	57	46	59
7	Southampton	38	15	10	13	71	63	55
8	Wimbledon	38	13	16	9	47	40	55
9	Nottingham Forest	38	15	9	14	55	47	54
10	Norwich City	38	13	14	11	44	42	53
11	Queens Park Rangers	38	13	11	14	45	44	50
12	Coventry City	38	14	7	17	39	59	49
13	Manchester United	38	13	9	16	46	47	48
14	Manchester City	38	12	12	14	43	52	48
15	Crystal Palace	38	13	9	16	42	66	48
16	Derby County	38	13	7	18	43	40	46
17	Luton Town	38	10	13	15	43	57	43
18	Sheffield Wednesday	38	11	10	17	35	51	43
19	Charlton Athletic	38	7	9	22	31	57	30
20	Millwall	38	5	11	22	39	65	26

SQUAD: Franz Carr, Lee Chapman, Gary Charles, Steve Chettle, Nigel Clough, Gary Crosby, Mark Crossley, David Currie, Sean Dyche, Gary Fleming, Colin Foster, Tommy Gaynor, Scot Gemmill, Lee Glover, Steve Hodge, Nigel Jemson, Roy Keane, Brian Laws, Andy Marriott, Toddy Orlygsson, Garry Parker, Stuart Pearce, Brian Rice, John Sheridan, Phil Starbuck, Steve Sutton, Justin Walker, Des Walker, Darren Wassall, Brett Williams, Terry Wilson, Ian Woan,

1990/91

Sat 25 Aug 1990	Queens Park Rangers	H	League	D 1-1
Tue 28 Aug 1990	Liverpool	A	League	L 0-2
Sat 01 Sep 1990	Coventry City	A	League	D 2-2
Sat 08 Sep 1990	Southampton	H	League	W 3-1
Sat 15 Sep 1990	Crystal Palace	A	League	D 2-2
Sat 22 Sep 1990	Arsenal	H	League	L 0-2
Wed 26 Sep 1990	Burnley	H	LC 2R 1L	W 4-1
Sat 29 Sep 1990	Manchester United	A	League	W 1-0
Sun 07 Oct 1990	Everton	H	League	W 3-1
Wed 10 Oct 1990	Burnley	A	LC 2R 2L	W 1-0
Sat 20 Oct 1990	Chelsea	A	League	D 0-0
Sat 27 Oct 1990	Tottenham Hotspur	H	League	L 1-2
Wed 31 Oct 1990	Plymouth Argyle	A	LC 3	W 2-1
Sat 03 Nov 1990	Leeds United	A	League	L 1-3
Sat 10 Nov 1990	Aston Villa	A	League	D 1-1
Sat 17 Nov 1990	Sunderland	H	League	W 2-0
Sat 24 Nov 1990	Derby County	A	League	L 1-2
Wed 28 Nov 1990	Coventry City	A	LC 4	L 4-5
Sat 01 Dec 1990	Luton Town	H	League	D 2-2
Sat 15 Dec 1990	Queens Park Rangers	A	League	W 2-1
Sat 22 Dec 1990	Sheffield United	A	League	L 2-3
Wed 26 Dec 1990	Wimbledon	H	League	W 2-1
Sat 29 Dec 1990	Manchester City	H	League	L 1-3
Wed 02 Jan 1991	Norwich City	A	League	W 6-2
Sun 06 Jan 1991	Crystal Palace	A	FAC 3	D 0-0
Sat 12 Jan 1991	Coventry City	H	League	W 3-0
Sat 19 Jan 1991	Southampton	A	League	D 1-1
Mon 21 Jan 1991	Crystal Palace	H	FAC 3 R	D 2-2
Mon 28 Jan 1991	Crystal Palace	H	FAC 3 2R	W 3-0
Sat 02 Feb 1991	Crystal Palace	H	League	L 0-1
Wed 13 Feb 1991	Newcastle United	A	FAC 4	D 2-2
Sat 16 Feb 1991	Sunderland	A	League	L 0-1
Mon 18 Feb 1991	Newcastle United	H	FAC 4 R	W 3-0
Sat 23 Feb 1991	Aston Villa	H	League	D 2-2
Mon 25 Feb 1991	Southampton	A	FAC 5	D 1-1
Sat 02 Mar 1991	Luton Town	A	League	L 0-1
Mon 04 Mar 1991	Southampton	H	FAC 5 R	W 3-1
Sat 09 Mar 1991	Norwich City	A	FAC 6	W 1-0
Sat 16 Mar 1991	Manchester United	H	League	D 1-1
Wed 20 Mar 1991	Arsenal	A	League	D 1-1
Sat 23 Mar 1991	Everton	A	League	D 0-0

Sat 30 Mar 1991	Wimbledon	A	League	L 1-3
Mon 01 Apr 1991	Sheffield United	H	League	W 2-0
Sat 06 Apr 1991	Manchester City	A	League	L 1-3
Wed 10 Apr 1991	Derby County	H	League	W 1-0
Sun 14 Apr 1991	West Ham United	N	FAC SF	W 4-0
Sat 20 Apr 1991	Chelsea	H	League	W 7-0
Wed 24 Apr 1991	Norwich City	H	League	W 5-0
Sat 04 May 1991	Tottenham Hotspur	A	League	D 1-1
Mon 06 May 1991	Liverpool	H	League	W 2-1
Sat 11 May 1991	Leeds United	H	League	W 4-3
Sat 18 May 1991	Tottenham Hotspur	N	FAC Final	L 1-2

DIVISION ONE

1	Arsenal	38	24	13	1	74	18	83
2	Liverpool	38	23	7	8	77	40	76
3	Crystal Palace	38	20	9	9	50	41	69
4	Leeds United	38	19	7	12	65	47	64
5	Manchester City	38	17	11	10	64	53	62
6	Manchester United	38	16	12	10	58	45	59
7	Wimbledon	38	14	14	10	53	46	56
8	Nottingham Forest	38	14	12	12	65	50	54
9	Everton	38	13	12	13	50	46	51
10	Tottenham Hotspur	38	11	16	11	51	50	49
11	Chelsea	38	13	10	15	58	69	49
12	Queens Park Rangers	38	12	10	16	44	53	46
13	Sheffield United	38	13	7	18	36	55	46
14	Southampton	38	12	9	17	58	69	45
15	Norwich City	38	13	6	19	41	64	45
16	Coventry City	38	11	11	16	42	49	44
17	Aston Villa	38	9	14	15	46	58	41
18	Luton Town	38	10	7	21	42	61	37
19	Sunderland	38	8	10	20	38	60	34
20	Derby County	38	5	9	24	37	75	24

SQUAD: Gary Bowyer, Franz Carr, Gary Charles, Steve Chettle, Nigel Clough, Gary Crosby, Mark Crossley, Tommy Gaynor, Scot Gemmill, Philip Gilchrist, Lee Glover, Steve Hodge, Bobby Howe, Nigel Jemson, Roy Keane, Ian Kilford, Brian Laws, Tony Loughlan, Andy Marriott, Toddy Orlygsson, Garry Parker, Stuart Pearce, Brian Rice, John Sheridan, Phil Starbuck, Steve Sutton, Carl Tiler, Justin Walker, Des Walker, Darren Wassall, Brett Williams, Terry Wilson, Ian Woan,

1991/92

Sat 17 Aug 1991	Everton	H	League	W 2-1
Tue 20 Aug 1991	Leeds United	A	League	L 0-1
Sat 24 Aug 1991	Notts. County	A	League	W 4-0
Wed 28 Aug 1991	Tottenham Hotspur	H	League	L 1-3
Sat 31 Aug 1991	Oldham Athletic	H	League	W 3-1
Wed 04 Sep 1991	Manchester City	A	League	L 1-2
Sat 07 Sep 1991	Sheffield Wednesday	A	League	L 1-2
Sat 14 Sep 1991	Wimbledon	H	League	W 4-2
Sat 21 Sep 1991	Aston Villa	A	League	L 1-3
Wed 25 Sep 1991	Bolton Wanderers	H	LC 2R 1L	W 4-0
Sat 28 Sep 1991	West Ham United	H	League	D 2-2
Sat 05 Oct 1991	Queens Park Rangers	A	League	W 2-0
Tue 08 Oct 1991	Bolton Wanderers	A	LC 2R 2L	W 5-2
Sat 19 Oct 1991	Sheffield United	A	League	L 2-4
Sat 26 Oct 1991	Southampton	H	League	L 1-3
Wed 30 Oct 1991	Bristol Rovers	H	LC 3	W 2-0
Sat 02 Nov 1991	Norwich City	A	League	D 0-0
Sat 16 Nov 1991	Coventry City	H	League	W 1-0
Sat 23 Nov 1991	Crystal Palace	H	League	W 5-1
Sat 30 Nov 1991	Chelsea	A	League	L 0-1
Wed 04 Dec 1991	Southampton	H	LC 4	D 0-0
Sun 08 Dec 1991	Arsenal	H	League	W 3-2
Sat 14 Dec 1991	Liverpool	A	League	L 0-2
Tue 17 Dec 1991	Southampton	A	LC 4 R	W 1-0
Sun 22 Dec 1991	Leeds United	H	League	D 0-0
Thu 26 Dec 1991	Tottenham Hotspur	A	League	W 2-1
Sat 28 Dec 1991	Oldham Athletic	A	League	L 1-2
Wed 01 Jan 1992	Luton Town	H	League	D 1-1
Sat 04 Jan 1992	Wolverhampton Wanderers	H	FAC 3	W 1-0
Wed 08 Jan 1992	Crystal Palace	A	LC 5	D 1-1
Sat 11 Jan 1992	Notts. County	H	League	D 1-1
Sun 19 Jan 1992	Everton	A	League	D 1-1
Sun 26 Jan 1992	Hereford United	H	FAC 4	W 2-0
Sat 01 Feb 1992	Sheffield United	H	League	L 2-5
Wed 05 Feb 1992	Crystal Palace	H	LC 5 R	W 4-2
Sun 09 Feb 1992	Tottenham Hotspur	H	LC SF 1L	D 1-1
Sat 15 Feb 1992	Bristol City	H	FAC 5	W 4-1
Sat 22 Feb 1992	Chelsea	H	League	D 1-1
Sun 01 Mar 1992	Tottenham Hotspur	A	LC SF 2L	W 2-1
Tue 03 Mar 1992	Crystal Palace	A	League	D 0-0
Sat 07 Mar 1992	Portsmouth	A	FAC 6	L 0-1
Wed 11 Mar 1992	Coventry City	A	League	W 2-0
Sat 14 Mar 1992	Norwich City	H	League	W 2-0
Wed 18 Mar 1992	Manchester United	H	League	W 1-0

Sat 21 Mar 1992	Manchester City	H	League	W 2-0
Tue 31 Mar 1992	Arsenal	A	League	D 3-3
Thu 02 Apr 1992	Wimbledon	A	League	L 0-3
Sat 04 Apr 1992	Sheffield Wednesday	H	League	L 0-2
Wed 08 Apr 1992	Southampton	A	League	W 1-0
Sun 12 Apr 1992	Manchester United	N	LC Final	L 0-1
Tue 14 Apr 1992	Luton Town	A	League	L 1-2
Sat 18 Apr 1992	Aston Villa	H	League	W 2-0
Mon 20 Apr 1992	Manchester United	A	League	W 2-1
Wed 22 Apr 1992	Liverpool	H	League	D 1-1
Sat 25 Apr 1992	Queens Park Rangers	H	League	D 1-1
Sat 02 May 1992	West Ham United	A	League	L 0-3

DIVISION ONE

1	Leeds United	42	22	16	4	74	37	82
2	Manchester United	42	21	15	6	63	33	78
3	Sheffield Wednesday	42	21	12	9	62	49	75
4	Arsenal	42	19	15	8	81	46	72
5	Manchester City	42	20	10	12	61	48	70
6	Liverpool	42	16	16	10	47	40	64
7	Aston Villa	42	17	9	16	48	44	60
8	Nottingham Forest	42	16	11	15	60	58	59
9	Sheffield United	42	16	9	17	65	63	57
10	Crystal Palace	42	14	15	13	53	61	57
11	Queens Park Rangers	42	12	18	12	48	47	54
12	Everton	42	13	14	15	52	51	53
13	Wimbledon	42	13	14	15	53	53	53
14	Chelsea	42	13	14	15	50	60	53
15	Tottenham Hotspur	42	15	7	20	58	63	52
16	Southampton	42	14	10	18	39	55	52
17	Oldham Athletic	42	14	9	19	63	67	51
18	Norwich City	42	11	12	19	47	63	45
19	Coventry City	42	11	11	20	35	44	44
20	Luton Town	42	10	12	20	38	71	42
21	Notts County	42	10	10	22	40	62	40
22	West Ham United	42	9	11	22	37	59	38

SQUAD: Craig Armstrong , Kingsley Black, Gary Bowyer, Gary Charles, Steve Chettle, Nigel Clough, Gary Crosby, Mark Crossley, Tommy Gaynor, Scot Gemmill, Philip Gilchrist, Lee Glover, Bobby Howe, Nigel Jemson, Jason Kaminsky, Roy Keane, Ian Kilford, Brian Laws, Andy Marriott, Paul McGregor, John Moncur, Toddy Orlygsson, Garry Parker, Stuart Pearce, Teddy Sheringham, Phil Starbuck, Steve Stone, Steve Sutton, Carl Tiler, Justin Walker, Des Walker, Darren Wassall, Brett Williams, Terry Wilson, Ian Woan.

1992/93

Sun 16 Aug 1992	Liverpool	H	League	W 1-0
Wed 19 Aug 1992	Sheffield Wednesday	A	League	L 0-2
Sat 22 Aug 1992	Oldham Athletic	A	League	L 3-5
Sat 29 Aug 1992	Manchester United	H	League	L 0-2
Mon 31 Aug 1992	Norwich City	A	League	L 1-3
Sat 05 Sep 1992	Blackburn Rovers	A	League	L 1-4
Sat 12 Sep 1992	Sheffield Wednesday	H	League	L 1-2
Mon 21 Sep 1992	Coventry City	H	League	D 1-1
Wed 23 Sep 1992	Stockport County	A	LC 2R 1L	W 3-2
Sat 26 Sep 1992	Chelsea	A	League	D 0-0
Sat 03 Oct 1992	Manchester City	A	League	D 2-2
Wed 07 Oct 1992	Stockport County	H	LC 2R 2L	W 2-1
Sat 17 Oct 1992	Arsenal	H	League	L 0-1
Wed 21 Oct 1992	Middlesbrough	H	League	W 1-0
Sat 24 Oct 1992	Sheffield United	A	League	D 0-0
Wed 28 Oct 1992	Crewe Alexandra	A	LC 3	W 1-0
Sat 31 Oct 1992	Ipswich Town	H	League	L 0-1
Sat 07 Nov 1992	Everton	H	League	L 0-1
Sat 21 Nov 1992	Crystal Palace	A	League	D 1-1
Sat 28 Nov 1992	Southampton	H	League	L 1-2
Wed 02 Dec 1992	Tottenham Hotspur	H	LC 4	W 2-0
Sat 05 Dec 1992	Leeds United	A	League	W 4-1
Sat 12 Dec 1992	Aston Villa	A	League	L 1-2
Sun 20 Dec 1992	Wimbledon	H	League	D 1-1
Mon 28 Dec 1992	Tottenham Hotspur	A	League	L 1-2
Sun 03 Jan 1993	Southampton	H	FAC 3	W 2-1
Sat 09 Jan 1993	Coventry City	A	League	W 1-0
Tue 12 Jan 1993	Arsenal	A	LC 5	L 0-2
Sat 16 Jan 1993	Chelsea	H	League	W 3-0
Sat 23 Jan 1993	Middlesbrough	H	FAC 4	D 1-1
Wed 27 Jan 1993	Manchester United	A	League	L 0-2
Sat 30 Jan 1993	Oldham Athletic	H	League	W 2-0
Wed 03 Feb 1993	Middlesbrough	A	FAC 4 R	W 3-0
Sat 06 Feb 1993	Liverpool	A	League	D 0-0
Sat 13 Feb 1993	Arsenal	A	FAC 5	L 0-2
Sat 20 Feb 1993	Middlesbrough	A	League	W 2-1
Wed 24 Feb 1993	Queens Park Rangers	H	League	W 1-0
Sat 27 Feb 1993	Manchester City	H	League	L 0-2
Wed 03 Mar 1993	Crystal Palace	H	League	D 1-1
Sat 13 Mar 1993	Everton	A	League	L 0-3
Wed 17 Mar 1993	Norwich City	H	League	L 0-3

Sun 21 Mar 1993	Leeds United	H	League	D 1-1
Wed 24 Mar 1993	Southampton	A	League	W 2-1
Sun 04 Apr 1993	Aston Villa	H	League	L 0-1
Wed 07 Apr 1993	Blackburn Rovers	H	League	L 1-3
Sat 10 Apr 1993	Queens Park Rangers	A	League	L 3-4
Mon 12 Apr 1993	Tottenham Hotspur	H	League	W 2-1
Sat 17 Apr 1993	Wimbledon	A	League	L 0-1
Wed 21 Apr 1993	Arsenal	A	League	D 1-1
Sat 01 May 1993	Sheffield United	H	League	L 0-2
Sat 08 May 1993	Ipswich Town	A	League	L 1-2

PREMIER LEAGUE

1	Manchester United	42	24	12	6	67	31	84
2	Aston Villa	42	21	11	10	57	40	74
3	Norwich City	42	21	9	12	61	65	72
4	Blackburn Rovers	42	20	11	11	68	46	71
5	Queens Park Rangers	42	17	12	13	63	55	63
6	Liverpool	42	16	11	15	62	55	59
7	Sheffield Wednesday	42	15	14	13	55	51	59
8	Tottenham Hotspur	42	16	11	15	60	66	59
9	Manchester City	42	15	12	15	56	51	57
10	Arsenal	42	15	11	16	40	38	56
11	Chelsea	42	14	14	14	51	54	56
12	Wimbledon	42	14	12	16	56	55	54
13	Everton	42	15	8	19	53	55	53
14	Sheffield United	42	14	10	18	54	53	52
15	Coventry City	42	13	13	16	52	57	52
16	Ipswich Town	42	12	16	14	50	55	52
17	Leeds United	42	12	15	15	57	62	51
18	Southampton	42	13	11	18	54	61	50
19	Oldham Athletic	42	13	10	19	63	74	49
20	Crystal Palace	42	11	16	15	48	61	49
21	Middlesbrough	42	11	11	20	54	75	44
22	Nottingham Forest	42	10	10	22	41	62	40

SQUAD: Craig Armstrong , Gary Bannister, Kingsley Black, Steve Blatherwick, Gary Bowyer, Gary Charles, Steve Chettle, Nigel Clough, Colin Cooper, Gary Crosby, Mark Crossley, Scot Gemmill, Lee Glover, Steve Guinan, Danny Hinshelwood, Bobby Howe, Roy Keane, Ian Kilford, Brian Laws, Andy Marriott, Paul McGregor, Ray McKinnon, Toddy Orlygsson, Stuart Pearce, Robert Rosario, Teddy Sheringham, Steve Stone, Carl Tiler, Justin Walker, Des Walker, Neil Webb, Brett Williams, Terry Wilson, Ian Woan.